Nativity Plays for Children

Nativity Plays for Children

Celebrating Christmas through Music and Movement

Wilma Ellersiek

Floris Books

Translated by Kundry Willwerth

First published in German under the title *Hirten- und Königsspiele*
by Verlag Freies Geistesleben, Stuttgart
This English edition published 2014 by Floris Books
Translation © Floris Books 2014

Wilma Ellersiek has asserted her right under the
Copyright Act 1988 to be identified as the
Author of this work

Introductory essays reproduced by kind permission
of the Waldorf Early Childhood Association of North America

British Library CIP Data available
ISBN 978-178250-116-9
Printed and bound by Gutenberg Press Limited, Malta

Contents

Introduction

Thirty-five years ago, Wilma Ellersiek began the process of creating her two Christmas plays. This book, long-awaited by educators, allows us to preserve her plays for future generations. The plays have been in their present form since 1998. They have undergone many transformations in an ongoing effort to render these simple scenes as artistically as possible through the use of rhythm and music.

Wilma Ellersiek succeeded in expressing nature's life energy (of plants and animals, of the appearances of sun, moon and stars, wind and water, snow and rain, thunderstorms and seasonal occurrences) through countless small, imaginative hand gestures and stories. This expression of the energy of nature is especially well developed in these Christmas plays. Through speech, rhythm and melos (mood of the fifth melodies), the vital aspects of nature's life energy are played out in a way that children can enjoy. These concerns, combined with the Christ impulse arising from this labour of love, have resulted in these plays.

The plays are designed so that there are no disruptions due to envy or jealousy triggered by allocating roles, no 'cute' costumes, and no intellectually detached observation. Through full immersion and communal participation in the games, what would otherwise simply be remembered stories become a joyful and nourishing Christmas experience in the here and now.

In kindergartens and playgroups, as well as in workshops for parents and teachers, I have often seen how a fluid circle is created through joint participation. In the centre of these activities – as shepherds receiving the heartwarming message of the angel; hurrying full of anticipation to the stable; in amazement and reverence at finding the child in the manger; and then, in a loose circle, with swinging movements rocking the child back and forth – the child in the manger becomes the sunlight of the heart. The experience flows into gestures of Mary and Joseph's thankfulness, and the child answers with a smile, reflected in the faces and hearts of the children.

The shape of the Three Kings Play is quite different. Everything becomes an illuminating guide to show the way. The star that all follow, the child on the throne, and the giving of thanks are all depicted in a natural and joyful manner. The two plays, through the combination of inner meaning and outer creativity – adapted to suit children – hold the potential to move hearts and minds.

By dramatising the quest for inner warmth and peace, and a more individual quest for the spiritual guiding star, the plays allow children to experience and engage with the world through movement and sound.

I know from the feedback I have received from my workshops that the Shepherds and Kings plays are often worked on and learned by heart in the warmth of the summer sun. It was no different for me: I worked on them on the beach of Elba, in Italy. It requires weeks (if not months) of preparation to fully immerse oneself in these complex plays so that even the smallest gestures are learned, while connecting with them as works of art. If possible, it can be helpful to work with members of the Wilma Ellersiek Hand Gesture Games Work Group who offer workshops and training and are happy to offer guidance.

When one considers how young children's sensory development links to their openness towards imitation, one can only hope that this book finds the widest distribution. Heartfelt gratitude is therefore extended to Ingrid Weidenfeld, dedicated and personal student of Wilma Ellersiek, who shepherded this publication so expertly.

Jacqueline Walter

Jacqueline Walter is a Waldorf kindergarten teacher in Rheinfelden, Switzerland. At the special request of Wilma Ellersiek, she gave a workshop on these plays at the international kindergarten conferences in Dornach in 1998 and 2005, along with Kundry Willwerth, who translated this book.

General notes

These stories for Christmas and Epiphany, in the form of simple plays with hand and body gestures and musical suggestions, are primarily conceived with early childhood and pre-school ages in mind. They are role-changing, simple identification plays, in which nobody is cast into a special part. That is to say, each child plays every role while the play evolves. These stories with gestures are not meant to be performed as plays in front of an audience. Rather, each story is complete in itself, with everyone participating.

The stories are in rhyming verse, with songs and music in the mood of the fifth, as part of the dramatic action; there is a unified action of speaking and movement. The storyteller is both a player, and the dramatist–speaker. Even the handing out of instruments is included in the play, so the action itself will not be interrupted.

The children do the actions at the same time as the storyteller – the action led is the action imitated. Everyone moves in unison throughout the play. There are no groups set aside for special attention. Everything is done in the circle with free, unhindered gestures, which over the course of the play create the characters and objects.

- Thus, all the children will kneel as shepherds before the crib.
- All will be Mary or Joseph.
- All, as ox and donkey and sheep, will warm the child with their breath.
- All as shepherds will dance round the crib.
- All as angels will protect the child, etc.
- The same principle holds for the whole action in the Three Kings Play.

The children continually change roles, slipping into each in turn, experiencing what is essential in the characters and the entire drama. The experience of the whole becomes meaningful, simply through taking part. This procedure is a truly creative experience.

No special conditions or demands interrupt or detract from the unity of this experience, coming as it does through participation in all gestures, movement, speech and tone. The whole group will be carried by the swing of the same rhythmic stream; the whole group will be united and moved by the same vibrating sounds. The working of the word is experienced as an event of movement and sound.

The following games may be performed not only by educators in the kindergarten, but also by parents – after some preparation – with their children. It is good for parents to have a practical introduction to the play's action. Through this they may step away from abstract concepts and sentimental images, and into the spirituality of the simple gestures. Thereby they are able to immerse themselves into the creative world which is the primary home of the child in the first seven years of life. But above all, this allows them to enjoy creating the play together with their children at home.

Play-acting together also has an important social function. It brings the family together in the Advent, Christmas and Epiphany seasons. Friends and neighbouring families can also take the opportunity to meet and visit each other for this common act of celebration. As there is no need for scenery or costumes, and a small soft-ringing bell can easily substitute for finger-cymbals, it is possible to perform these stories at any time.

Depending on the group and the space available, the play may take either the complete or the core form. Many young parents who may no longer have any connection to the traditional forms, text or songs here, can gain a new engagement with Christmas and Epiphany by play-acting together with their children.

Rhythmic–musical games

Rhythmic-musical games are an artistically created play opportunity for the first seven years of life. This combination form, as I have developed it, is an opportunity for play in which things are not brought to children in a direct or naturalistic way, but rather in an artistically rendered form, using gestures, poetic speech, and mood of the fifth melodies that lift children to the level of universal truths. Introduction to objective order, rather than a projection of subjective experience, is an important factor in child development. The combination play form evolves from this.

Rhythmic-musical games go beyond the usual practice of assembling, grouping and combining methods of play. They are a 'finished composition' that develops into a fantasy-rich 'whole'. This allows children to experience the individual aspects of things – of nature, of people, and even of their naturally occurring connections. This is transmitted in a pulsing-swinging action, both rhythmical and musical, in which the children can wholly immerse themselves. In this way they start to experience, engage with and embody the world.

In this method, reality is represented through various small and large gestures that capture its essence. This reality is further developed through words in the form of appropriate poetic language (rhythmic and rhyming verses). Through imitation, the children dip unconsciously into this imaginative play by following the adult's example.

This kind of play helps children's holistic development in the first seven years of their life, as it helps them develop meaningful relationships with nature (seasons, days, life situations, natural events). This allows them to experience the sheltering bosom of 'Mother Earth'. From the feeling of security that this creates, children become less fearful, and the injuries they receive through exposure to the adult world can be healed.

Rhythmic-musical games, with their creative gestures and movement, offer children in the first seven years of life the opportunity to 'breathe' and the ability to find themselves. This is achieved through the possibility of slipping into (and nestling within) an orderly and harmonising structure, which accompanies children on their path as they continue to develop.

Paul Hindemith expressed it like this:

> World harmony, harmony of the world,
> is the rule, the order, that we fail to
> recognise. Therefore seek to bring into
> the world the awareness of this rule,
> this order, which expresses hope.

For children in the first seven years of life, this consciousness of world harmony is a 'bodily knowing'. It is transmitted through gestures, and through the imitation of gestures that have been acquired and incorporated.

Language as music

The following notes come from the book *Music and Rhythm Among the Greeks* by Thrasybulos Georgiades, and are extended through additions by Wilma Ellersiek.

In Greek times – that is, from ancient times

up until the end of the fifth century AD – music was exclusively connected with speech. In fact, it was so well connected with speech that strictly speaking, the term 'Greek music' cannot be justified. There was, of course, instrumental music, but music as an all-embracing phenomenon did not exist independently. It was understood not in isolation, but as only one part of a totality: one aspect of language ability; of speech; of poetry; one aspect of that reality that is called μουσικη (*musiké*). That which we call music has its origin in this *musiké*. 'Choir' meant to the ancient Greeks a unity of singing and dancing to verse. Only later was this term (chorus) used exclusively for singing.

As Thrasybulos Georgiades writes:

> That which music and speech have in
> common, that in which the unity of
> music and language is also expressed,

is the rhythm. The speech chorus, which was danced, also provided the rhythm for the dance. Thus speech, poetry, music and dance are united by rhythm...

This certainly suggests that they are to be seen as a unity - a unity 'that had its roots in the particular talents, the particular mental attitude of the Greeks. (...) Speech is the etheric parent of language, (...) is (not just art), but spiritual being as such.'

This experience of language as music and spiritual being corresponds to the experience of the growing child in the first seven years.

The tabard

The tabard is a ceremonial garment used in the plays for children aged one to seven. Through wearing the tabard, a joyful and expectant mood becomes established in the children. The garments provide the children a certain defence against distracting surroundings. This helps children take part in the plays without feeling exposed or 'special'. In a sense, a protective space is formed.

As shape and colour of the tabard is the same for all children taking part, a feeling of one common body arises, providing a good basis for the dramatic form, in which all participants perform the same action together. The neutral tabards mean there is no need for certain characters being determined by particular costumes. Rather it gives participants the chance to portray any character or anything at all through gestures.

The neutral, uniform costuming, together with the experience of all performing at the same time, means that every participant's contribution is equally valued.

Children who have been involved in plays in the past with assigned roles and costumes have been shown to cope well with the dramatic form without costumes, if wearing the tabard. But it is also possible to abandon all special costumes; for the children experience the action through gestures. So an outer garment is not really necessary, when the children are totally absorbed in the creative action and feel comfortable in it.

Those who wish to use colourful tabards may use basic colours or rainbow colours that are light and transparent. Silk, wool-silk or light cotton material is suitable. A simple coloured or golden belt will enhance the festive feeling for the children.

When using coloured tabards it is important that the children get the colour they desire so as to avoid feelings of envy. Some disharmony in colours may be unavoidable. Often the best solution is the same colour tabard for all participants. As the tabard is a neutral, festive garment, its colours have no direct influence on the play action. Green colours are associated with life-giving forces. Bright yellow or gold colours encourage the experience of light. Red colours are linked to empowerment of movement. Blue colours support an awareness of air and of breathing (an important part of the gestures during the play action).

All this happens without the child being aware of it. But colours in their basic form may be included as a complement to the creative aspects of the action.

Sewing instructions for the tabard are on page 169.

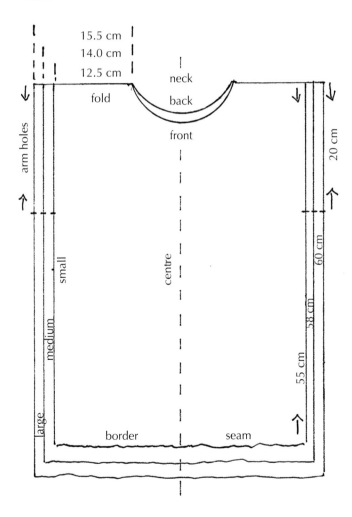

Children's participation in the plays

Give the children plenty of time to get used to imitating the movements, speech and gestures in the plays. Different personalities will naturally respond differently to the experience.

- The predominantly *sense-directed* child will take longer in the stage of wonder, of taking it all in, and will gradually come to the point of playing along.
- The mainly *active* child will quickly adopt the gestures and enter into the action, only speaking and singing later.
- The predominantly *acoustic* child will be among the first to enter into the speaking and singing.
- The predominantly *tactile* child greatly enjoys all touching games. She will enjoy stroking the lamb and making the ox's horns, the donkey's ears or the sheep's hooves with satisfaction. She will also like playing the musical instruments, carrying and packing and unpacking the basket, etc.
- The *intellectual* child has a hard time entering into the action and identifying with the characters. At first she will simply watch what is going on, and will often make precociously clever comments.
- The *chaotic* child may find it hard to fit her unrestrained will into the orderly gestures – she will often stray from the action.
- The *precocious* child will try to dominate the action with her interpretation and opinions, only slowly being able to enter the rhythm of the action unselfconsciously.
- The *hypersensitive* or *overstimulated* child will turn away because she is too easily overwhelmed.
- The *edgy* or *irritable* child will refuse, because she can only be reached slowly and with patience.

After a number of repetitions you will find that all the children say the texts and sing the songs together and happily make the gestures together. (Children who do not yet do this in the kindergarten often will repeat it at home). What is important is that the adult unites herself with the action of the play and truly engages with the gestures of movement, speech and tone.

One thing I must note: whatever is proffered to the children in the Shepherds or Three Kings plays, or in the other plays, is a gift from the spirit world in a creative form. What works spiritually in speech and body gestures is something into which children, but also the person educating them, can submerse themselves – like into a 'curative' bath. There are both children and grown-ups who live in that spiritual element naturally. Others only enter in haltingly, and some may even refuse.

In that case: patience! Those who refuse to take part may be very unhappy, for they would be only too glad to participate, but life and environment have already placed barriers in their way, which one must carefully dismantle and help to place in order. This can happen simply through participation in these plays. Through rhythm and tune, they carry the ordering element of the creative to the child.

It is important not to become irritated by the behavior of reluctant or disruptive children, who most especially need this help. Don't regard these difficulties as 'disturbances': simply avoid showing an angry reaction. We must feel deep compassion with these children who have been

traumatised by their environment. Only one thought should motivate us – to help them find their way to the healing spring, to the water and bread of life from which they have been cut off.

Have no expectations; do not in any way express what the child is expected or required to do. Let the child sit quietly or play somewhere by herself. On the other hand, always keep the child in your consciousness throughout the whole proceeding. There will be moments in which the child's attention is caught, when she may even come over and want to join in. Jingle sticks or bells-on-rings may be the lure; the child may want to be the donkey and the bird with the others. Maybe she will want to join in the singing. Increasingly, the child is drawn into what is being done. It is like a release.

Co-workers must lend each other strength in sustaining this approach, so that it can bear fruit. The problems will recede, and may even be solved. A peacefulness enters that fills both child and educator with joy and thanks, and gives them strength to solve the next problem.

Speaking and singing

Rhythmic-musical speech and singing in family and kindergarten are activities particularly suitable to the young child. However, patience is needed to train the speaking and singing voice so it can sound like a 'musical instrument'. Such speech/song must be called forth through the rhythm and melos of speech. Speech as movement and sound experience are of primary importance. Content, meaning and concept are secondary. Singing must produce an instrumental, unemotional sound without emphasising the singer's own sentiments.

In these plays, the literal meaning retreats into the background; the child should be presented

with the rhythmic-musical and dynamic action of the language. The pliability of the sounds, the rhythmic pulse of the stream of language, the melody of sounds, the variety of 'tone hues', the dynamic of the volume – these are what must engage our attention. Our speech nearly sings; it is lifted up and away from the prosaic. We must avoid the conventional 'sing-song' interval of the third, which can sound too close to the patterns of speech. Instead, the sound is made to *correspond* with speech, where a variety of pitch and timbre arise, defying conventional musical notation. Thus the creative, artistic spirit of the language, rather than its conceptual aspect, comes to the fore. By immersing themselves in the process of forming sounds, and in making word-gestures together with the adult, children come to know the form through which the language arises. This is archetypical gesture (movement) rather then mere abstract concept. In the ongoing process the children can embody the language within themselves and thus undergo a profound, comprehensive spiritual shaping. In this formative process both speech and language have a creative function. The child's organism itself is moulded (brain development etc.), and the foundation is built for the creative, imaginative use of language.

In terms of singing, it needs to be mentioned that the adult should approach the child very carefully with lullabies and melodic motifs. Singing should be *sotto voce* without vibrato. The tone should glide on the breath stream, surrounding, rather then gripping the child. The rocking movement and the singing of the words must be embedded in a pulsating flow. The singing is not meant to impress, but to form a shelter into which the child can nestle. To do this, all sentimentality and emphasis on the textual meaning is best avoided.

All songs in the mood of the fifth start with the central note: A. It is important that the educator actually starts the songs at this pitch. A is the sun tone, around which the tones of the mood of the fifth are grouped in a wonderfully harmonic order. The tone space from D to E, that is, the interval of the ninth, corresponds ideally to the range of a child's voice.

Since few people are blessed with perfect pitch, it is good to tune in before singing with the help of an instrument. Especially suitable for this are the Choroi instruments, particularly the one-hole flute with the intervals D–A. When you blow into it without covering the hole, you hear the A. The interval flute is easy to play. One blows on the breath-stream, without additional tonguing (no 'tut-tut', as with a recorder). The tone, gently breathed, has a comforting effect; it touches the child like a gentle caress. The soft, diffuse tone of the Choroi instruments fits the child's constitution; the sound remains in the outer space and leaves the child free.

One should only use the Choroi flute if one can produce this gentle tone easily. Otherwise it is better to sing, but this also must be done carefully and quietly, not with the full voice. Neither the recorder nor the concert flute are recommended for the pre-school age. Their resonance-rich sound and direct tone affect the sensitive constitution of the young child, and make too strong an impression on them. Other suitable instruments like brass sound-tubes, pentatonic flute or children's harp also give the tone A in a soft sound.

After the educator has obtained the tone from an instrument, she hums it softly to the group. This gets the children into the right pitch for singing. A single note from the flute (or harp, or brass tone bar) then becomes a natural starting point for the opening of the play.

Rhythm and pulsation

The feeling of rhythm in the first seven years is fundamental, based on pulsation. Pulsation is the initial element, the root of all rhythmic activity. It is the constant repetition of what is similar, yet not identical. Pulsation is the basic beat, oriented to the heartbeat, dividing the stream of time.

Pulsation has two aspects. It is the polarity between stress and relief, impulse and relaxation (usually denoted as 'pause' or 'rest'), in which something decisive occurs, namely the preparation for another impulse. The heartbeat also has two parts: a polarity of expansion and contraction (sytabard and diatabard). In the same way, breathing has its polarity of exhalation and inhalation. Like pulse and breathing, pulsation is variable in tempo; like these, it has the ability to adjust and can become slower or faster, thus working as an enlivening element in time's flow.

The musical notation used here is not one of fixed, measurable values. It is meant as a memory aid for the various melodies. Sing freely, follow the motion of language and movement, without necessarily being bound by long or short notes or time beat.

The conventional notation of songs separated into bars is avoided here so as not to hinder the pulsating stream of the melody. All notes are written without the usual stems, and bars are not marked. Already, when viewing the two different notations, one can see that notation bound by bars is firm and structured, while the free notation without bars or note stems represents the streaming flow of movement, speech and melody.

In the notation used here, the conventional four-quarter count is marked as the four notes in a pulsation: •••• or o.

Hand gestures

The gestures have to be formed through careful observation. They must be broken down into their constituent parts, so that they can be reproduced. Through hand gestures, observations of reality can be reproduced physically, and in an artistic (not naturalistic) manner.

Precise imagination (as Goethe calls it) works in a formative way. One escapes the subjective perception, the emotional, into the process of objective observation ('receiving the truth') of the phenomena. This way of observing is the basis for the creation of phenomenologically fitting representative gestures. Through gesture that is oriented in the basic phenomenon, an experience of cosmic order can be obtained, working in the earthly sense perception of creation.

Taking account of early childhood and pre-school experiences, it must be our task to take the path from basic phenomenon to basic gesture. The basic gesture, then, can be used in creating rhythmic-musically formed gesture games, which express the action in verses and mood of the fifth songs.

For educators

Ideally, the adult who sings and speaks with children trains and cares for her voice. She also needs to work on her movements, so that they are a good example for the children. If, because of physical problems, one cannot assume sitting on one's heels or the knee-stand without great difficulty, one can perform these gestures standing. It is better to move freely than in a cramped way because of pain.

The same is true for singing; if it is not possible to easily and freely sing the songs in the noted tone, then it is better to speak the text rhythmic-musically, stressing rhythm and melos. The actual textual meaning is then subordinated to the sound action. Children experience such melodious speaking as music. It is also possible to exchange the high E with the B; easy singing is important.

The Shepherds Play

The Shepherds Play

The Core Play

It is a good thing to introduce children to the play slowly, rather than trying to perform the whole play at once.

First of all, the *Ding-dong song* can become part of the kindergarten morning. The first verse of this song is suitable if preparing for the Shepherds Play, but it may also be sung in the run-up to Christmas with the children. It becomes part of the daily routine. The important thing is that they hear the mood of the fifth. It is up to the children whether they want to sing along. They receive no encouragement to sing. With a good teaching model and frequent repetition, this happens by itself. The second verse is sung at the end of the play or after December 24th.

Then the hand-gesture song *Be still, keep quiet...* (p. 28) should be sung. This song is actually the core piece of the play (from the 'Angels guard the child' part of the structure). It is important that it takes the central position and is played with the children first. Whether the Core Play or Complete Play is chosen, *Be still, keep quiet...* must be part of it.

As time goes on, Supplementary Scenes may be inserted into the Core Play, so that the children grow into the Complete Play without stress. For older children, the new additions will be an exciting surprise. The educator must have a sense for what is appropriate depending on the age group, social configuration and spatial possibilities.

For the very young, or for children with disabilities, the Core Play is recommended. It is also suitable for playing in the family circle at home. The basic structure of its composition is:

- Tuning in
- Annunciation
- The shepherds come
- In the stall
- Diddle-doh dance and It-is-enough song
- Angels guard the child
- The shepherds leave
- Conclusion

The Play circle

The ideal play formation is a circle of stools, next to an open area as a 'field', from which all move to the stable and back. It is also effective to use the stool circle for all the play events, especially with younger children or if room is limited. If there is no room for the stool (or chair) circle, all can play sitting on heels on the floor. This is appropriate for the Shepherds Play, since shepherds spend much of the time on the ground. However, the ordering function of the stool circle for the play action cannot be substituted easily.

The manger with the child is in the centre of the play space, covered with a cloth in the beginning. The educator and the children sit, stand and move in the circle around it.

The rocking of the child in the play is not a realistic event, but a symbolic act, so a suggestion of the manger in the centre is sufficient – for example, hay and straw on a cloth on the floor. See suggestions for the manger (p. 170).

The Shepherds Play: Overview

Preparation

- Building of the play circle (set up stool or chair circle)
- Arranging manger with child (covered)
- Preparing basket with musical instruments
- Preparing treats
- Dressing children in festive tabards, if using

The Core Play

A. DING-DONG SONG (TUNING IN)

B. WE BEGIN (SILVER CYMBALS OR BRASS BELLS)
'We begin' and 'Conclusion' are always accompanied by finger cymbals or a small brass bell.

1. Annunciation
2. The shepherds come
   Supplementary Scene 1:
      Up the hill, down the hill
3. In the stall: Adoration
               Rocking
               Animals warm the child
4. Diddle-doh dance and It-is-enough song
   Supplementary Scenes 2–6:
      Rest-diddle-doh
      Sound of the silver cymbals
      Jingle sticks
      Knock-knock sticks
      Call of the animals
5. Angels guard the child (hallowing)
6. The shepherds leave
   Supplementary Scenes: *The complete closing* and *Up the hill, down the hill*
7. Return of the shepherds

C. IT IS DONE

D. TREATS
After the play, the children receive something sweet to chew, like hazelnuts or raisins, so they are permeated by a physical well-being. In this way the play action even affects their metabolism.

The Shepherds Play (Core Play)

A. Ding-dong song (tuning in)

1. Ding-dong! Ding - dong! Dong - dong! Ding - dong! Ding - dong!
2. Ding-dong! Ding - dong! Dong - dong! Ding - dong! Ding - dong!

1. Bells are swing - ing, bells are ring - ing, hear their tune!
2. Bells are swing - ing, bells are ring - ing, far and near.

1. Hear their tune! Call - ing, call - ing: the Christ Child comes soon!
2. From near and far, call - ing call - ing, the Christ Child is here!

1. The Christ child comes soon! Ding - dong! Ding - dong!
2. The Christ Child is here! Ding - dong! Ding - dong!

1. Ding - dong! Ding - dong! Dong - dong! Ding - dong! Ding - dong!
2. Ding - dong! Ding - dong! Dong - dong! Ding - dong! Ding - dong!

B. We begin

We be - gin – we be - gin

1. ANNUNCIATION

In the meadow, with their sheep
are the shepherds who sleep – sleep.
Only two the watch must keep
to guard that they lose no sheep.
Appears an angel in the night,
they all awake from his glorious light.
Full of amazement they hear him sing,
news of great joy the angels bring.
The angel chorus now rejoice:
Come, oh shepherds, one and all
to the manger in the stall.
Come and see – come and see
what this great wonder be!

A litt - le child is born in Beth' lem in the stall,
the cho - sen of our Fath-er, to bring great joy to all,

to bring great joy to all.

The angel chorus now rejoice:

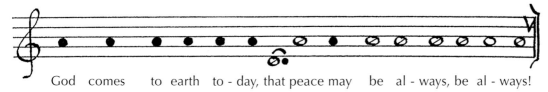

God comes to earth to - day, that peace may be al - ways, be al - ways!

2. THE SHEPHERDS COME

See, the shepherds, coming all,
all are coming to the stall,
there to see, there to see,
what this great wonder be.
Sheep and lambkin, trip-trip-trong
with the shepherds come along.
Sheep and lambkin, trip-trip-trong
with the shepherds come along.

Hurry all – hurry all
to Bethlehem, to the stall,
there to gaze – there to gaze
at the wonder that's taken place.
Stand in amaze!

3. IN THE STALL

Adoration
Arrived are all by the stall,
by the stall.
Enter here – enter here,
find within the baby dear.

Sheep and shepherds by the manger
standing there in great amaze
in joy upon the heavenly child
now gaze.
Bend their knees low,
bow their heads so
before the child of God on high
whom to visit they came by.

Rocking
See him lie on straw and hay.
And with Mary and with Joseph
they the baby rock and sway.

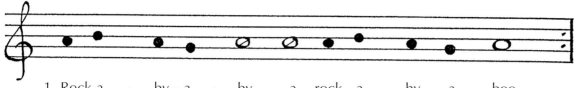

1. Rock-a - by - a - by - a, rock - a - by - a - boo,
2. Rock-a- - by - a ba - by, we are rock - ing you!

1. Rock-a - by - a - by - a, rock - a - by - a - boo,

2. Rock-a- - by - a - boo, we are ro - cking you, you, you.

Mary and Joseph say: "Thank you all,
for your rocking, rocking. Thank you all!"
And the baby smiles so dear, smiles so dear,
that their hearts turn warm with cheer, warm with cheer!

Animals warm the child
Ox and donkey and the sheep
gathered also by the manger
with their breath – haah!
with their breath – haah! – haah!
Baby Jesus warm they keep.
And Mary and Joseph say: "Thank you all!
For your warming, thank you all!"
And the baby smiles so dear, smiles so dear,
that their hearts turn warm with cheer, warm with cheer!

4. DIDDLE-DOH DANCE AND IT-IS-ENOUGH SONG

All the shepherds are joyful and gay.
They dance around the manger a round-a-lay.

1. Did - dle didd - le   didd - le - do,   all   a - round the   ring   we go,
2. Did - dle didd - le   didd - le - do, jum - ping round the   ring   we go,

1. Round and   round we   go, aye, didd - le didd - le - do,   aye,
2. Round and   round we   go, aye, didd - le didd - le - do,   aye,

1. Didd - le   didd - le - do,   round we   go, round we go!
2. Didd - le   didd - le - do,   round we   go, round we go!

Then Joseph calls: "Stop awhile!
It is enough now for the child."
So the shepherds stop a bit
and quietly sit,
quietly.

Joseph sings:

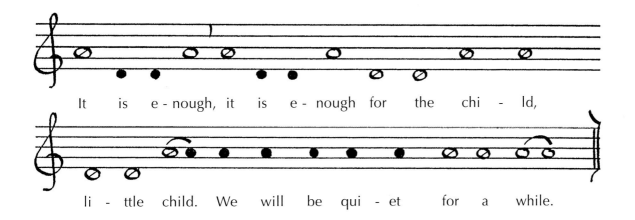

It is e - nough, it is e - nough for the chi - ld,

li - ttle child. We will be qui - et for a while.

5. ANGELS GUARD THE CHILD (HALLOWING)

And the beautiful, bright angels
coming hither from on high
all the beautiful, bright angels
guard the child as they draw nigh.

Be still, keep qu - iet, the ba - by wants to sleep.

Ma-ry sings her child to sleep. Ox and don-key and the sheep

all are near the crib in the stall. And angels, angels, an-gels guard him all.

Be still, keep qui - et, the ba - by wants to sleep.

Jo - seph rocks the child to sleep. Ox and don-key and the sheep

all are near the crib in the stall. And angels, angels, an-gels guard him all.

Be still, keep qui - et, the ba-by wants to sleep, quiet, quiet, quiet.

He slumbers deep – the baby sweet,
and in his sleep he smiles so dear,
smiles so dear
that the heart turns warm with cheer,
warm with cheer.
And Mary and Joseph say: "Thank you
bright angels, for your guarding: thank you!"

6. THE SHEPHERDS LEAVE

Today the shepherds, in the stall
saw the holy Christ Child dear.
With their sheep together all
must walk back to the pasture near.
They go with gladdened heart.

All the shep-herds and their sheep go to the field in mea-sured tread. The

heaven - ly won - der they have met!

Yes, the ba - by smiles so dear, the ba - by smiles so dear,

that the heart turns warm with cheer! Cheer! Cheer!

7. Back in the Pasture

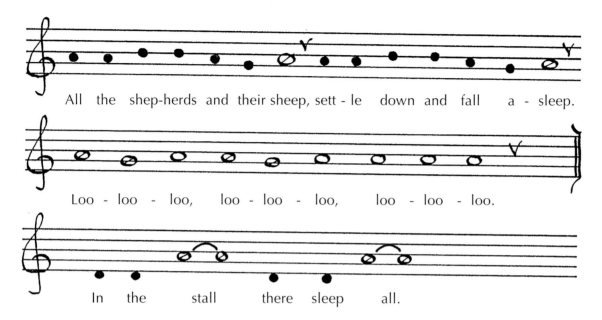

All the shep-herds and their sheep, sett - le down and fall a - sleep.

Loo - loo - loo, loo - loo - loo, loo - loo - loo.

In the stall there sleep all.

Back in the pasture with their sheep
all sit down to sleep.
Guarded by the angels bright
in the high, holy night,
in the Christmas night.

C. It is done

It is done, it is done!

D. Treats

At the end we have some treats.
Jesus each one fondly greets.
Open up! I'll give you one.
Chewing, chewing! Mmm – yum, yum!

The Shepherds Play: Directions

Speaking must be formed so that the speech can be perceived as a movement and sound experience. Allow time to prepare for all movements. The creative process is more important than the finished gesture. It is important for all gestures and movements that there is sufficient space so that the children don't bump each other. If necessary, simply make smaller movements.

A. Ding-dong song (see p. 22)

The educator leads the singing children into the play space. At the end of the song the group forms a circle and sits down on the floor or on stools (or chairs.) If the route is rather long, the song may be repeated until everyone has taken their place on the floor. The educator gets the cymbals for the beginning.

B. We begin (see p. 23)

The educator strikes the cymbals gently, and, as in the picture, moves them up slowly while listening to the sound. She moves them outward and then sings *We begin!* as their sound fades. She repeats this, then puts the cymbals away.

We   be - gin –   we   be - gin

1. ANNUNCIATION

Text

1. *In the meadow...*

       ← →

Movement

1. The educator sits on her heels on the floor and the children in a circle around her. (Another version: all sit on stools or chairs, arranged in a circle.) After the beginning call, the educator raises her hands slightly at about stomach height, palms facing down. With her hands she points forward and to the sides in a wide arc, showing the meadow. The movement is very slow. She draws out the word *meadow*. The children imitate or watch, without being encouraged to participate.

2. *With their sheep…*

2. The educator places her hands above her chest as legs, her fingers bent down as hooves. She nods twice as she says the word *sheep*.

3. *are the shepherds…*

3. Now the educator wraps her arms in a large arc around her head with the left arm on the outside, visible to the observer. She rests her forehead on her right arm.

4.   *and sleep – sleep.*

4.   The educator bends slowly forwards with her arms wrapped around her forehead. The word *sleep* is drawn out and in the same pitch, almost like singing. She holds the gesture for a moment.

5.   *Only two the watch must keep…*

5.   At *only*, the educator sits up, putting both hands like a shield over her eyes. This is the symbolic gesture for the watchful shepherd. She looks watchfully across the field. At *two* she turns a little toward the left, and at *watch* a little toward the right.

6.   *to guard the herd…*

6.   The educator takes her hands from her forehead and moves them in front of her chest with palms down, to make a protecting gesture. Silently, she holds the gesture a little longer.

7. *That they lose…*

7. At *that* the educator forms her left hand into a loose fist and rests it as a lamb's head against her breast bone. She covers it with her right hand. Then she strokes the lamb's head lovingly (again, with her right hand).

8. *not one sheep…*

8. The educator speaks the words *not one* very slowly, so there is lots of time for caressing.

9. *Appears an angel in the night…*

9. The educator kneels while moving her arms up as wings, palms toward the audience (the symbolic movement for the angel may be made kneeling or standing).

10. *They all awake...*

10. The educator rubs her eyes with both hands. Then she moves her hands to the sides next to her head while looking up to the sky in amazement.

11. *from his glorious light...*

11. Now the educator moves her 'wings' a apart a little, slightly higher and also a little further back. It is a quiet movement in three directions.

12. *Full of amazement they hear him sing.*

12. The educator moves her raised arms and hands a little in front of her head. Her right hand is raised a little higher than her left, palms toward the audience. Surprised, and seeking protection from the brightness, she listens toward heaven.

13. (Silent movement)

13. The educator lowers her arms and stands up, but keeps her amazed/listening gesture.

14. *News of great joy the angels bring…*(see p. 23)

14. Standing, the educator makes the wing gesture from before. At *the angels bring*, she bends her wings slightly forward. Then she begins to sing (see music).

15. *A little child is born…*

15. At *born*, the educator lifts her arms, to the side and backwards a little. This is a wing beat, as seen before.

16. *in Beth'lem in the stall…*

16. The educator brings her hands together in front of her forehead to show a round roof. The fingers of her right hand lie on top of the fingers of her left hand.

17. *The chosen of our Father…*

17. A wing beat (see instruction 9, on p. 36).

18. *to bring great joy to all…*

18. The educator moves her hands down and together, her hands, palms down, meet in front of her stomach. At the word *joy*, she swings up her hands a little.

19. *To bring great joy to all.*

19. Now the educator turns her hands, palms up. She moves them apart horizontally, as if to distribute something or to point to everything. She does not spread her hands too far apart.

20. *The angel chorus now rejoice...*

20. The educator holds her lower arms at right angles. Then, at breast height, she begins to turn her hands enthusiastically while moving them upwards. At *rejoice* she stands with arms held high, palms to the audience, in front of the onlooker.

21. *God comes to earth today...*(see p. 23)

21. All sing again. She makes the movements as in instruction 18. She lowers her arms and spaces the words *God comes to earth...* evenly. At *earth*, she makes a light, swinging movement upwards with her hands.

God comes   to earth to - day, that peace may   be al - ways, be al - ways!

22. *that peace may be always!*

22. The educator spreads her hands, palms down, apart and then together again. At *always*, she holds the joint hands in a blessing gesture.

23. *Come, oh shepherds, one and all...*

23. The educator turns joyfully to the children. At the words *come* and *one* and *all* she waves the shepherds to her, from the middle, the left, and right.

24. *to the manger in the stall...*

24. At the word *manger* the educator bends down a little and forms a bowl at thigh height. At *stall* she straightens up again and makes a round stable roof with her hands, as in instruction 16.

25. *Come and see – come and see...*

25. The educator continues with the roof gesture, but takes it a bit higher and further away. From underneath she looks far away, twice in the same direction, stretching a little at the second *come and see.*

26. *what this great wonder be!*

26. The educator moves her hands, which are nearly touching, upwards and out in a circle. At *wonder* she reaches maximum height. Only after the word *wonder* does she open her hands and arms. Very slowly, she brings down her arms and hands. In front of her belly she forms a bowl, and at *be* she holds this bowl in front of her as a symbol for a gift received.

2. THE SHEPHERDS COME

1. *See*

1. With her right hand held high (without overstretching the arm) the educator turns happily to the children.

2. *the shepherds, coming all...*

2. With her arm raised high she invites the children to Bethlehem with a great, all-inclusive arc from right to left.

3. *all are coming to the stall*
   there to see, there to see
   what this great wonder be.

3. The educator turns her left shoulder to the circle centre and walks clockwise along the circle, beginning with the left foot, starting the journey to the stable. She does not follow the beat; this is not a march. Pauses are inserted between the lines while all continue to walk. Speech will become more intense, perhaps even louder, towards the word *wonder*, which should be pronounced slowly.

4. *Sheep and lambkin, trip-trip-trong*
   with the shepherds come along.

4. The educator places her hands above her chest as legs, her fingers bent down as hooves. She trips along with small steps, pulling her knees up lightly with each step (see picture). Again, the tripping steps should not match the rhythm of the words. This may happen occasionally, but should not be done continuously. The children need not walk exactly on the circle line; they may move freely.

Supplementary Scene *Up the hill, down the hill* can be added here – see p. 64

5. *Hurry all – hurry all…*

5. The educator dissolves the lambkin gesture and continues in a light smooth run. Each time, at the word *hurry* she makes a spirited action with her hands and arms parallel from back to front, as if to drive the herd along. (When running silently there is no arm movement.)

6. *to Bethlehem, to the stall…*	6. She continues to run and at the words *to the stall* she repeats the driving action once more. At *Bethlehem* she continues to walk along the circle, pointing forward.
7. *there to gaze – there to gaze at the wonder that's taken place. Stand in amaze!*	7. As she continues walking, the educator repeats the arm movement from *hurry*. For the word *wonder* she swings her arms forward once more from the back – this time as high as her head. Then she lowers her arms, slows down the walking and eventually comes to a standstill. She allows enough time until all are standing still. Then she says the final words: *stand in amaze!*

3. In the Stable

Adoration

1. *Arrived are all…*	1. The educator makes a quarter turn toward the circle centre and waits until all the children have done so too.
2. *by the stall, by the stall…*	2. She then shows the stable roof as in instruction 16 (see p. 38). She keeps the roof gesture and confirms it with a nod at the second *by*, bending gently forward and then straightening up again.

3. (Silent)	3. Now the educator releases the roof gesture and looks at the children.
4. *Enter here – enter here…*	4. At *enter*, she softly steps to the middle with her right foot, then repeats another step with her left foot. If there is not enough room, she places the left foot next to the right foot. (If a circle of stools or chairs is there, then this is the moment to step between the stools into the inner circle.)
5. (Silent)	5. If there is a helper, then he or the educator now takes away the cloth that covered the child (or just draws it back).
6. *find within the baby dear…*	6. The educator remains in her place, but bends her upper body slightly toward the child and stretches her arms forward (her elbows remain slightly bent). Her palms face towards each other, as if she would like to pick the child up.
7. *Sheep…*	7. At *sheep* she puts her hands as hooves against her chest and nods twice.

and shepherds…

At the word *shepherds* the educator places both hands as a shield against her forehead. She speaks slowly and takes her time forming the gestures.

standing there in great amaze…

At *amaze* she takes a small step backwards, clasping her hands softly together and then resting them on her chest. She remains in this position for a little while.

8. *in joy upon the heavenly child now gaze…*

8. Now she loosens her hands and moves them upwards in an arc. At the word *child* she has reached the highest point (see picture), while looking up to heaven. Then she takes her arms slowly downward and, with palms upward, points to the child in the manger as if to say: 'from high heaven he came to us!' With this gesture, she looks at the child fondly.

9. *Bend their knees low...*	9. The educator kneels down. Her shins should be on the floor, her body is straight above the knees.
10. *bow their heads so* *before the child of God on high*	10. She now lowers her head, lightly crossing her hands on her chest. She remains in this position until *on high*.
11. *whom to visit they came by...*	11. During this text the educator straightens up slowly – her hands remain crossed on her chest.

Rocking

1. *See him lie on straw and hay...*	1. The educator lowers herself into the knee stand and then sits on her heels. Simultaneously, she moves her hands down and rests them on her knees, while looking at the child for a while.
2. *and with Mary...*	2. She puts her hands together (as in prayer), bends forward a little and moves her hands slightly downward.

3. *and with Joseph…*

3. Symbolic gesture for Joseph: the educator rests her chin on her crossed hands (see picture). She remains in this position for a while. Imagine Joseph leaning on his staff. His hands rest on its crook.

4. *they the baby rock and sway…*(see p. 25)

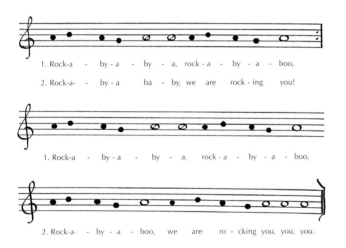

1. Rock-a - by - a - by - a, rock - a - by - a - boo,
2. Rock-a- - by - a ba - by, we are rock - ing you!

1. Rock-a - by - a - by - a, rock - a - by - a - boo,

2. Rock-a- - by - a - boo, we are ro - cking you, you, you.

4. The educator releases the gesture, imagines the cradle at about stomach height and lets it swing back and forth with soft pressure from her hands. The note A is sounded. She rocks in the rhythm of the song (as marked with arrows). The movements are very small; no wild swinging. The movement comes from the wrist. The ball of the hand moves forwards and back as if one was pressing lightly against a cradle. It is a symbolic gesture for weaving between those who came and the Jesus child. A communication! God offers us his love, we offer him ours. If the movement stays directed, a 'mandala' of children's hands can begin around the cradle. Pause at the end.

Note: It is important to find the right tempo for rocking. This is not a lullaby to fall asleep to, as in *Be still, keep quiet.…* The shepherds communicate what they have heard of the child. The child will bring joy to all, the Savior has come! The 'tidings of joy' must be shown, though the movement is restful, not hurried.

5. *Mary and Joseph say: "Thank you all…"*	5. When speaking the names, the educator shows each symbolic gesture for Mary and Joseph (see instructions 2 and 3). At *thank you* she opens her arms and hands towards the front and moves them down with a small bow.
6. *For your rocking, rocking. Thank you all!"*	6. The educator performs the rocking movement twice more, each time to the word *rocking*. She says *thank you* as in direction 5.
7. *And the baby smiles so dear, smiles so dear…*	7. The educator moves her hands close to her body, palms up, at about stomach height. She leaves a small distance between her hands, holding each hand separately, like a little bowl. By *smiles so dear, smiles so dear* she gently rocks her hands in the gesture described.
8. *that their hearts turn warm with cheer, warm with cheer…*	8. At *warm* she rests both hands on her heart. For the repetition, keep this gesture and at *warm*, nod as if to say *yes*!

Animals warm the child

1. *O…*	1. The educator speaks a long drawn-out *O*, the beginning of the animal's name, while moving her hands slowly up to her forehead. She forms fists, which, at the *x* in ox, she lays at the edges of her forehead, thumbs down, to signify horns. She gently bends her head.

2. *and donkey…*

2. She now opens her fists, turning them forwards (palms to the audience). The *o* in donkey is drawn out like the *o* in *ox*. At the same time, she stretches her upper body slightly.

3. *and the sheep…*

3. The educator brings her hands downwards while bending her elbows. At *sheep* she places them on her chest as hooves. At *and* and *sheep*, she nods.

4. *gathered also by the manger…*

4. The educator gets on hands and knees, supporting herself with her fists on the floor. This is not meant as a naturalistic animal portrayal, but one needs to be very close to the Jesus child to warm him.

5. *with their breath – haah!*
    their own breath – haah! – haah!

5. At *haah* the educator moves her head forward, towards the child. She breathes the breath as quietly as possible. ('Breathed' breath is warm, 'blown' breath is cooler!)

6. *Baby Jesus warm they keep…*

6. The educator sits back on her heels. She crosses her arms, pressing them tightly against her chest and rubs her upper arms as if to show that it is cold.

7. *Mary and Joseph say: "Thank you all!*

7. Slowly, the educator forms the symbolic gestures for Mary and Joseph, and at *thank you* she opens her hands forward, moving them down with a small bow.

8. *"For your warming: Thank you all!"*

8. At the word *warming* she crosses her arms, pressing them tightly against her chest and rubs her upper arms. *Thank you* is done as in instruction 5 on p. 47.

9. *And the baby smiles so dear, smiles so dear…*

9. For movements, see instruction 7 on p. 47.

10. *that their hearts turn warm with cheer, warm with cheer.*

10. For movements, see instruction 8 no p. 47.

4. DIDDLE-DOH DANCE AND IT-IS-ENOUGH SONG (SEE P. 26)

1. *All the shepherds are joyful and gay…*

1. The educator stands up with a joyful bounce. She times her speaking so that at *joyful* she can raise her arms.

2. *They dance around the manger a round-a-lay…*

2. Now she turns with her right shoulder to the circle centre and begins walking in a circle (depending on the age group or group dynamic, the participants may also hold hands).

3. & 4. 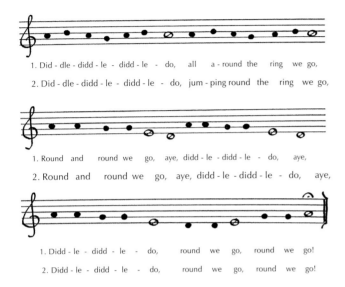 (see p. 26)

1. Did - dle - didd - le - didd - le - do,   all   a - round the   ring   we go,
2. Did - dle - didd - le - didd - le - do,   jum - ping round the   ring   we go,

1. Round and   round we   go,   aye,   didd - le - didd - le - do,   aye,
2. Round and   round we   go,   aye,   didd - le - didd - le - do,   aye,

1. Didd - le - didd - le - do,   round   we   go,   round   we   go!
2. Didd - le - didd - le - do,   round   we   go,   round   we   go!

5. *Then Joseph calls:*

6. *"Stop awhile!*

7. *It is enough now for the child."*

3. The educator gives the A note and sings the first verse of the *Diddle-doh dance* while walking in the pulsation rhythm around the manger, without any special stress as she sings and walks.

4. The educator continues singing the verse, skipping lightly in the same direction. (If the group members were holding hands, they should let go now.) Skipping will vary according to age – it could be galloping etc. – let the children choose. Coordination of speech and movement is not yet suitable for the children. The educator articulates the words clearly while singing, and they give the impulse to the movement. The dance becomes livelier and ends with a final jump, both feet together.

5. Quickly, the educator takes on the role of Joseph, who raises his right hand as if to give a signal.

6. She lowers her raised arm a little, then moves her hand forward, bent back as if to signify stopping, at *Stop awhile!* She holds this gesture for a few seconds.

7. The educator releases the gesture. She moves her hand down slowly, palm down, as if to protect the child while speaking mildly and comfortingly in a very melodious tone. At *for the child* she keeps her voice suspended. She continues the protecting gesture for a little while.

8. *So the shepherds stop a bit and quietly sit.*

8. The educator makes an inviting gesture in an arc from right to left and moves away from the manger a little so that the play circle expands slightly. At the word *quietly* she lowers herself by bending her knees.

9. *Quietly.*

9. She lowers herself fully to sit on her heels, resting her hands flat on her thighs. She remains this way for a while.

10. Joseph sings (see p. 27):

It is e - nough, it is e - nough for the chi - ld, li - ttle child. We will be qui - et for a while.

10. The educator makes the symbolic gesture for Joseph, holds it a moment, and then begins to sing after she tunes to the note A.

11. *It is enough, it is enough…*

11. The educator makes a calming gesture with both hands, palms toward the audience, first to the left, then to the right.

12. *for the child, little child…*

12. Then she turns her hands, palms down, and moves them downwards in a protecting gesture for the child in the manger.

13. *We will be quiet for a while.*	13. The educator moves her hands to her mouth and at the end puts her fingertips against her upper lip. She holds this gesture for a while.

Note: The *It-is-enough song* can also be played on a pentatonic Choroi flute or a Choroi-interval flute D–A.

The Supplementary Scenes 2–6 may be inserted here.

2. *Rest-diddle-doh* (see p. 67)
3. *Sound of the silver cymbals* (see p. 69)
4. *Jingle sticks* (see p. 74)
5. *Knock-knock sticks* (see p. 79)
6. *Call of the animals* (see p. 82)

5. Angels guard the child (Hallowing)

1. *And the beautiful, bright angels…*	1. The educator rises on to her knees, lifting her arms across her front to make the angel gesture.

2. *coming hither from on high…(front)*	2. She moves her arms (wings) forward slightly, making a soft wing beat.
3. *all the beautiful, bright angels…(back)*	3. She swings her arms back again (wing beat backwards) and moves them forward a little.
4. *guard the child as they draw nigh…*	4. Now the educator moves her hands down holding them over the manger in blessing. She remains in this position for a little while.

5. (Silent)	5. Silently, the educator sits back on her heels or sits down on a stool. She prepares the gesture for *be still*. With loose fingers, she holds her hands close together at chest height, palms forward. The idea is to create a sheltering space for the 'holy thing' present. Then she tunes to the A note and begins singing.

6. *Be Still...* (see p. 28)

Be still, keep qu - iet, the ba - by wants to sleep.

Ma - ry sings the chi-ld to sleep. Ox and don-key and the sheep

all are near the crib in the stall. And angels, angels, an-gels guard him all.

Be still, keep qui - et, the ba - by wants to sleep.

Jo - seph rocks the child to sleep. Ox and don-key and the sheep

all are near the crib in the stall. And angels, angels, an-gels guard him all.

Be still, keep qui - et, the ba-by wants to sleep, quiet, quiet, quiet.

6. At *Be still* the educator makes a similar gesture to the previous one, with both hands together, slightly turning to the left. At *quiet keep*, she moves to the right.

7. *the baby wants to sleep...*

7. The educator rests her head with her left ear on her flat, closed hands, shutting her eyes and swaying lightly back and forth.

54

8. *Mary sings her child to sleep...*

8. The educator makes the symbolic gesture for Mary, first kneeling upright then bowing towards the manger while singing.

9. *Ox and donkey and the sheep...*

9. While naming the animals, the educator makes the same gestures as on p. 47 and 48. She draws out the words *ox* and *donkey* slowly and nods her head at *and* and *sheep*.

10. *all are near the crib in the stall...*

10. The educator moves both hands forward, palms up, pointing to the crib. Her upper body follows the gesture gently.

11. *And the angels, angels...*
    (back)   (forward)   (back)

11. During the short pause, before the word *and*, the educator lifts her arms in the angel gesture and then, while singing, moves the 'wings' rhythmically back and forth.

12. *angels guard him all...*

12. Now she lowers the wings slowly, changes into the protecting gesture (see picture on p. 51) and holds them over the crib in blessing.

13. *Be still, keep quiet,*
    the baby wants to sleep!

13. See p. 54, instruction 6.

14. *Joseph rocks the child to sleep...*

14. The educator rocks the manger with both hands. With the balls of her hands she pushes the cradle gently and allows it to swing back.

15. *Ox and donkey...*

15. Preparation and execution of the gestures (see steps 9, 10, 11 and 12).

16. *Be still, keep quiet etc...*

16. See steps 6 and 7, on p. 54.

17. *Quiet – quiet – quiet…*

17. The educator moves to the first and second *quiet* as in instruction 6 from p. 54. For the third *quiet* she moves her hands in an outward arc then back to her mouth, resting her fingertips on her lips. She listens after the last tone, holding the same gesture. It is important that the singing pauses are observed. The gestures, however, must be connected fluidly.

18. (Silent)
He slumbers deep – the baby sweet.

18. After the last tone has faded away, the educator bends slightly down to the Jesus child and looks silently at him for a moment. Then she says *he slumbers…*

19. *And in his sleep he smiles so dear, smiles so dear…*

19. She moves her hands, palms up, towards the manger and swings them in parallel back and forth. This happens very gently, as if intending to caress the child.

20. *that the heart turns warm with cheer, warm with cheer…*

20. Movements as on p. 49.

21. *Mary and Joseph say: "Thank you!"*

21. Movements as on p. 48.

22. *"You bright angels, for your guarding: thank you."*

22. The educator makes the symbolic gesture for the angel, then lowers her hands to the guarding gesture as before. For *thank you* she spreads her hands sideways (see picture).

6. THE SHEPHERDS LEAVE

1. *Today the shepherds...*

1. The educator remains sitting on her heels touching her forehead with both hands – the symbolic gesture for watchful shepherds.

2. *in the stall...*

2. For the word: *stall*, she forms a roof again (see p. 38).

3. *saw the holy Christ Child dear...*

3. She releases the roof gesture by taking her arms forward in an arc down to the manger, then she points to the manger, palms upward.

4. *With their sheep...*

4. The educator holds her hands as hooves above her chest, nodding at *with* and *sheep*, with her head lightly bent.

5. *Together all...*

5. The educator gets up joyfully, arranging her speech so that *all* is said when she is standing. She now turns to the children.

5. (cont) *must walk back to the pasture near...*

5. (cont) At *walk* she nods in confirmation and then at the word *pasture*, with palms down, she spreads her hands wide (at stomach height).

6. *(Silent movement)*

6. Without speaking, she puts her hands on her heart. Holding this gesture, she bows before the Jesus child in the manger. Then she straightens up again.

7. *They go with gladdened heart...*(see p. 29)

7. Now the educator turns her right shoulder to the circle centre. She moves clockwise with arms and hands hanging down, walking in a circle. She tunes to A and starts singing.

8. *All the shepherds and their sheep...*

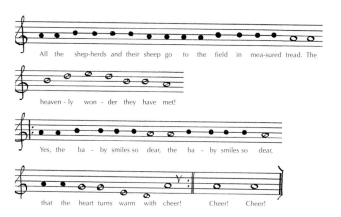

All the shep-herds and their sheep go to the field in mea-sured tread. The

heaven - ly won - der they have met!

Yes, the ba - by smiles so dear, the ba - by smiles so dear,

that the heart turns warm with cheer! Cheer! Cheer!

8. All move in a circle, singing. The children need not go exactly one behind the other. The educator walks freely; movement and singing need not coincide. The song can be repeated in whole or part as desired.

The following Supplementary Scenes may be inserted here.

Up the hill, down the hill
and/or
The complete closing

The play would then end with *The complete closing.*

7. BACK IN THE PASTURE

1. *Back in the pasture with their sheep...*

1. The educator slowly comes to a stop, waiting until the last child stops too.

2. *all sit down to sleep…(see p. 30)*

All the shep-herds and their sheep, sett-le down and fall a-sleep.

Loo - loo - loo,   loo - loo - loo,   loo - loo - loo.

2. At the word *sleep* she slowly sits down on her heels (or she sits down on a stool or chair).

3. *All the shepherds and their sheep, settle down and fall asleep.*
    Loo-loo-loo, loo-loo-loo, loo-loo-loo…

3. After everyone is sitting on their heels (or sitting on stools) the educator bends her head, resting her face in her hands. Then she begins to sing: *All the shepherds…* At the same time, she rocks to and fro. All happens very quietly and gently.

4. *In the stall there sleep all…*

In the stall there sleep all.

4. At the word *stall* the educator shows the roof gesture (see p. 38). At *all*, she lightly rests her forehead in her hands with her upper body bent forward slightly. She remains in this position for a while before releasing it.

5. *guarded by the angels bright…*

5. The educator rises on her knees while lifting her arms in the wing position (if sitting on a stool, she only raises her upper body).

6. *in the high, holy night…*
    (back) (forward) (back)

6. She swings the 'wings' exactly as marked under the words, back, forwards, then back again. The movement is very delicate.

7. *in the Christmas night...*

7. Now she lowers her arms forward in the gesture of blessing. She holds the gesture quietly for a while, then lets it go very slowly.

C. It is done

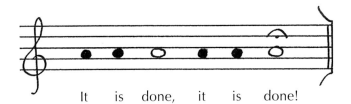

It   is   done,   it   is   done!

Before singing, the educator gently strikes the cymbal, moving her arms slowly forward and then apart to right and left and together. She sings into the dying sound: *It is done!* This is repeated.

D. Treats

At the ending there are treats.
Jesus each one fondly greets.
Open up – I'll give you one.
Chewing, chewing! Mmm – yum yum!

The educator gets the bowl of hazelnuts or dried fruit. She goes from child to child and puts a treat into each mouth (or hand). She repeats the verse until everyone has a treat.

Note: Experience has shown the advantage of giving the children something sweet to chew after the play, such as seedless prunes, a piece of apple, a few raisins or a nut. Then the children feel a physical well-being so that the play-action affects even their metabolism. Give the children plenty of time. The play-action then ends with the 'call for conclusion' followed by clean-up and the possible removal of the festive garments.

Call for conclusion

Our   shep - herds play   is   done,   we leave the   cir - cle   one   by   one.

Supplementary Scenes

To extend and supplement the core version of the Shepherds Play, there are seven Supplementary Scenes. By adding some of these, a large Shepherds Play is formed. If all Supplementary Scenes are included, the Complete Play is created.

The form of the Shepherds Play with the Supplementary Scenes can be very flexible. The main considerations are the physical space available, the kind of group playing, and the teacher's capacity.

1. *Up the hill, down the hill*
2. *Rest-diddle-doh*
3. *Sound of the silver cymbals*
4. *Jingle sticks*
5. *Knock-knock sticks*
6. *Call of the animals*
7. *The complete closing: Return of the shepherds*

The following Supplementary Scene can be inserted at: *With the shepherds come along…* (see Core Play p. 42) and/or in *The shepherds leave…* after the song *All the shepherds and their sheep* (see Core Play p. 58).

1. Up the hill, down the hill

Where up the hill the road has led
sheep and lambs go tread – tread –
tread.
tread – tread – tread – tread
nodding, nodding with their heads.
Tread – tread – tread.

Shepherds, too, they step and tread,
step – step – with firm tread,
tread – tread – tread.

When at last the road leads down
run the sheep all trup – trup – trown,
truppa – truppa – truppa – truppa,
truppa – truppa – trup – trup – trown.

Shepherds, also, run and run,
running, running, getting on,
just as fast as they can come.

Note: It is important that there is enough room so that the children can move without bumping into one another. Both children and educator move clockwise in a circle, but not exactly on the circle circumference. The number of steps and the speech pulsation need not coincide; walking in step may sometimes happen, but need not always be that way. On no account should it be requested.

Text

1. *Where up the hill the road has led…*

2. *sheep and lambs go tread – tread – tread.*
    tread – tread – tread – tread…

sheep and lambs go tread-tread-tread, tread-tread-tread-tread.

Movements

1. With her hand the educator makes an arc from bottom to top, diagonally, to show the hill she means to climb.

2. She holds her hands as front legs against her chest, bending her head forward a little. At *tread* she steps with her right foot (toes first) and for the sheep walking, she lifts her knees a bit higher than normal. She takes every step toes first. The walking speed should be a little slower then usual, as it goes uphill.

3. *nodding, nodding with their heads…*

      ^   ^   ^   ^

    tread – tread – tread.

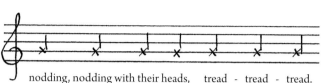

nodding, nodding with their heads,   tread - tread - tread.

3. At each [^] the educator nods her head lightly while walking.

4. *Shepherds, too, they step and tread,*
    step – step – with firm tread,
    tread – tread – tread.

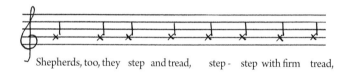

Shepherds, too, they step and tread,   step - step with firm tread,

4. Now she takes a few normal steps, then she speaks: *Shepherds, too...* Then she puts down her feet with heel first and walks 'up the hill' with firm steps (see left). The children do not need to walk in the speech rhythm!

5. *When at last the road leads down…*

5. This time the educator draws a line with her hand, diagonally, from top to bottom.

6. *run the sheep all trup – trup – trown,*
    truppa – truppa – truppa – truppa,

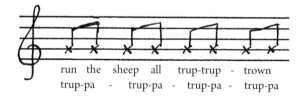

run the   sheep   all   trup-trup - trown
trup-pa - trup-pa - trup-pa - trup-pa

6. In the sheep gesture the educator moves in a light, loose run, knees a little high. On each *truppa* she takes two steps (see left).

truppa – truppa – trup – trup – trown.
run the sheep all trup - trup - trown

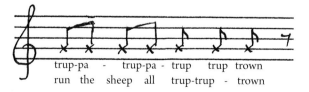

trup-pa - trup-pa - trup trup trown
run the sheep all trup-trup - trown

7.   *Shepherds, also, run and run...*

7.   Now the educator makes a few running steps without the sheep gesture, then she speaks: *Shepherds, also, run and run...*

8.   *running, running, getting on
     just as fast as they can come.*

8.   The educator moves in a running step, not too fast, in the speech rhythm. The lines may be repeated as needed.

running, running, getting on, just as fast as they can come

From here, the Core Play continues with *Hurry all, hurry all,*
see p. 41, or one can continue after the song:
All the shepherds and their sheep, p. 60.

Note: When Supplementary Scenes 3, 4 and 5 are not played, adding Supplementary Scene 1 both before and at the end of the Core Play is recommended.

The contrast of quiet steps and lively run is a simplified equivalent of the contrast of the long-lasting cymbal sound and the short ring of jingles. In this way, a musical aspect can be included into the play. It is also possible to include Supplementary Scene 1 only in the beginning. On the other hand, one should consider that for pre-school or restless children this game may have a 'release' function.

2. Rest-diddle-doh

(for the pentatonic Choroi flute)

This may be added after or instead of the *It-is-enough-song*. *Rest-diddle-doh* is a great preparation for *Angels guard the child*.

One of the good shepherds there
had the fine idea
to bring his shepherd flute
to play for the baby dear.
He plays the Rest-diddle-doh.
We all listen, too.

Mary and Joseph say:
"Thank you!
For playing your flute: Thank you!"
And the baby smiles so dear, smiles so dear,
that their hearts turn warm with cheer,
warm with cheer!

1. *One of the good shepherds there…* ∧ *had the fine idea…* ∧	1. The educator turns to the children as if to tell a story. She nods at the words *one* and *fine*.
2. (Silent)	2. Without a word, the educator takes the flute out of its cover or holder.

67

3. *to bring his shepherd flute...*	3. She lifts up the flute and shows it around.
4. *to play for the baby dear...*	4. Then she points slowly and gently to the child.
5. *He plays the* Rest-diddle-doh...	5. She lifts the flute to play it.
6. *We all listen, too.* (Educator plays the *Rest-diddle-doh*)	6. The educator uses a soft voice, placing her free hand behind her ear, so that the children start to listen. This is very desirable at this stage of the play. Then she plays the song on the flute. After the song the educator puts the flute down and shows the symbolic gesture for Mary (the same as in the short version).

7. *Mary and Joseph say: "Thank you!"*	7. The educator makes same gestures as in the short version, p. 47.
8. *"For playing your flute. Thank you!"* *And the baby smiles so dear, smiles so dear,* *that their hearts turn warm with cheer, warm* *with cheer!*	8. The educator plays for a moment on an imaginary flute. Then she continues as in the short version.

Continue the Core Play, or with a further Supplementary Scene
such as *Sound of the silver cymbals.*

Note about the flute music:
It is essential that the tone glides along the breath stream, if the desired state of quietness is to be attained. No tonguing should take place; the normal 'tut-tut' of the recorder should be avoided. Instead, one breathes in and blows gently along the length of the breath. This way of playing allows trouble-free movement from note to note. The whole melody has the character of the out-breath and creates a feeling of relaxation. One plays more slowly towards the end.

3. SOUND OF THE SILVER CYMBALS

This Supplementary Scene may be inserted after the *It-is-enough song* in the Core Play, or after *Rest-diddle-doh*. It is played sitting on your heels or on a stool.

One of the good shepherds there
had the fine idea
to sound for the little child
his silver cymbals here.
With them he plays for the Christ Child fair
softly a gentle cymbal air.

Silver cymbal sing 'Tinnnnng!'
Silver cymbal ring 'Tinnnnng!'
Cymbal sound takes time to ring
sound high 'Tinnnnng!'
sound wide 'Tinnnnng!'
swing into the outer sphere 'Tinnnnng!'
float up to the baby dear 'Tinnnnng!'
Gone the ringing –
gone the swinging.
The shepherd packs the silver cymbals away.
He puts them into their pocket case after the play.

Mary and Joseph say:
"Thank you!
For the 'Tinnnnng!' Thank you!"

And the baby smiles so dear, smiles so dear,
that their hearts turn warm with cheer,
warm with cheer!

1. *One of the good shepherds there
   had the fine idea…*

1. The educator turns to the children with the words *one of the good shepherds there*. Then she lifts up the case or the cloth with the cymbals and shows them to the children. Then she lays it quietly on her thighs and opens it.

2. *to sound...*

2. With thumb and index finger of her left hand she takes out a cymbal, holding it by its loop.

3. *for the little child...*

3. In the same way, at the word *child* she takes the other cymbal out with her right hand, also holding it by its loop.

4. *his silver cymbals here...*

4. At the word *his*, she places the cymbal she is holding on the right into the palm of her left hand (the loop pointing up) so that for a moment both cymbals lie in the left hand. Then the cymbal being held by the left thumb and pointer is placed in the palm of the right hand. The word *his* is spoken stretched out so that the action is performed rhythmically with the sound of the word. During the words *silver cymbals here* the educator moves her hands right around the circle, so that the children can look into her hands and see the cymbals.

5. *With them...*

5. She places the cymbals on her thighs.

6. *he plays...*

6. The educator lifts both hands lightly without the cymbals, pretending to strike them.

7. *for the Christ Child fair...*

7. At the words *Christ Child*, she takes the cymbal from her right thigh with her right hand (holding at the loop) and at *fair* she repeats the process with her left hand.

8. *softly a gentle cymbal air…*

8. The educator holds both cymbals close together in front of herself and at *softly*, she swings them together in a small arc towards the manger without the cymbals ringing. At *cymbal air* she swings the same arc back.

The ritual described here is an important event! It helps the child to find the transition from lively, rhythmic-musical dance and singing to listening in stillness without being directly instructed to do so. During her first seven years, the child lives primarily in the moving-musical experience. The ability to hear and to listen belongs to the sensory-musical and must be practised step by step. It should be asked of the child gently.

Also, in this action and its repetition (without special explanations), the child learns that an instrument must not lie around unprotected, as it might get damaged by light, air, warmth and cold. This is true for all instruments.

This ritual also includes the format of a rhythmic-musical play action, which gives extra importance to the uncovering and distribution of the instruments.

It is best not to skip the repetition of this action as, after a longer usage, it will become second nature. It must be understood that the repetition within the formed play action is a ritual that has a strengthening effect on the child's rhythmic system.

After the cymbals have been unpacked:

9. *Silver cymbal sing…* ⊖ ₁↑↑ ₂↓↓

9. The educator holds the cymbals next to each other and speaks to them in a very melodious tone, almost singing. At *cymbal* she strikes the left cymbal gently with the right cymbal from above. Then she moves the ringing cymbals straight up (1) and then down again (2) while listening to their sound attentively. Only after the sound of the cymbals has completely ceased does she continue.

* sign for cymbals ⊖

10. *Silver cymbal ring...*

10. After the words *silver cymbal ring* have been spoken, she strikes the cymbals again and, listening to their sound, moves them horizontally apart to right and left and together again.

11. *Cymbal sound takes time to ring sound high...*
and sound wide...

11. After striking, the educator moves the cymbals up again, following them with her eyes. When they are silent again she brings them back to chest height and tells them: *and sound wide*. Then she strikes the cymbals again, repeating the movements from the previous section. When all is silent she continues.

12. *Swing into the outer sphere...*

12. She makes a little circle with both cymbals, horizontally in front of herself.

13.

13. After striking, the educator moves both cymbals horizontally in a large circle, stressing the forward direction, while swinging the cymbals up and down. This creates a tone with a pulsing quality.

14. *Float up to the baby dear....*

(Silent movement)

14. Now she swings the cymbals in a small flat arc toward the manger and back again. Then she rises into a knee stand, moving her upper body towards the manger. She bends forward as if to bring the cymbals as close to the child as possible. At the same time, she moves the cymbals in four small circles along a spiral path toward the child.
She then holds the cymbals in front of the manger until they are silent. Then she takes the cymbals back and sits down, upright, on her heels.

15. *Gone the ringing – gone the swinging…*	15. Now the educator holds each cymbal up to an ear and listens.
16. *The shepherd packs the silver cymbals away. He puts them into their pocket case after the play.*	16. The educator takes the case or cloth, opens it, and at *puts* she pushes the first cymbal inside, and at *pocket case* inserts the second cymbal. The cymbals must not touch. (If a cloth was used, the text is: *She puts them in her cloth after the play.*)
17. *(She silently closes the pocket case and puts it aside.)*	17. The educator folds up the cloth (or closes the pocket case) and sets it aside.
18. *Mary and Joseph say: "Thank you! "*	18. See Core Play, p. 47.
19. *For the 'Tinnnnng!' Thank you!"*	19. At *Tinnnnng!*, sung by the educator for the first time, very light and soft, she strikes imaginary cymbals moving them straight up and down again.
20. *And the baby smiles so dear, smiles so dear, that their hearts turn warm with cheer, warm with cheer!*	20. See Core Play, p. 47.

4. JINGLE STICKS

*Craft directions for the jingle sticks are on p. 170.

This may be inserted after the *It-is-enough song* or after *Sound of the silver cymbals*.
Depending on which game preceded it, the title may be changed to *All of the good shepherds
there*. The game should be played on the floor, sitting on heels or on stools.

All of the good shepherds there
had a clever thought
and for the sounding for the child
their jingle sticks they brought.

They play with them clear and strong
for the dear child a jingle song.
Jingle sticks now:
shing-shing-shing-shing.
shinga-shinga-shinga-shing!
Jingle sticks now:
bing-bing-bing-bing.
Binga-binga-binga-bing!
Sound fine and clear
for the baby dear:
Shing-shing-shing-shing.
Shinga-shinga-shinga-shing!
Bing-bing-bing-bing.
Binga-binga-binga-bing!
Shing-shing-shing-shing.
Shinga-shinga-shinga-shing!

All the jingles quiet keep
for the baby wants to sleep.
Mary and Joseph say:
"Thank you!
For the 'shinga-shinga'! Thank you!"
And the baby smiles so dear, smiles so
dear,
that their hearts turn warm with cheer,
warm with cheer!

1. *All of the good shepherds there…*

1. The educator turns to the children.

2. *had a clever thought…*

2. She gets the basket with the jingle sticks.

3. *and for the sounding for the child…*

3. She shows the children the covered basket.

4. ^^^^^^^^^^^^ ^^^^^^^^

4. She shakes the basket so everyone can hear the bells.

5. *their jingle sticks they brought.*

5. She removes the cloth and one of the jingle sticks, and shows it to the children while shaking it happily.

6. *They play with them clear and strong…*

6. She tips the jingle stick lightly forward in the speech rhythm and at ^^^^^^^ shakes it.

7. *for the dear child a jingle song…*

7. In the speech rhythm she tips the stick lightly toward the manger.

8. *Jingle sticks now:*

8. The educator shakes the basket…

9. (Spoken)
For you ... for you ... for you ...etc (not in text above)

9. She walks around the circle passing out the jingle sticks, or she says: "each of you may take one out".

Handing out the jingle sticks is included in the game so that the total play process will not be interrupted.

If there are more than fifteen children present it is advisable to distribute jingle sticks from a second basket. This is introduced with: "I wonder, (insert child's name), would you like to help me hand out jingle sticks, too? You move this way (opposite direction) around the ring. And now we begin." Children ready for first grade will be delighted to take up such a task. So as to not disturb the peace the 'big ones' can determine whose turn it is to help before the play by counting: 'Eeny, meeny, miny mo...' In this way sadness or envy can be avoided. Of course younger children may also like to perform this special task. One can explain that the older children, who will go into first grade, are playing with us for the last time.

When the jingle sticks have been handed out and the basket put aside, the actual game with the jingle sticks begins.

Since the children have been playing with their jingle sticks during the distribution, quiet has to be established.

---

10. *All the jingles quiet keep...*

10. The educator lifts the jingle stick with her right hand and then grasps the jingles with her left hand.

11. (Silent movement)

11. and silently holds the covered stick to her right ear. She listens to the rolling of the small metal balls inside the jingle stick.

12. *for the baby...*

12. The educator continues holding the jingle stick to her ear and says softly *not anyone can hear them ding,* then she listens again for a short while.

13. *not anyone can hear them ding...*

13. At *not anyone* she shakes her head.

14. *Jingle sticks now:*
   Shing-shing-shing-shing.

   Shing-shing-shing-shing.

   Shinga-shinga-shinga-shing!
   ∧∧∧∧∧∧∧∧∧∧∧∧∧∧∧∧∧∧∧∧∧∧∧∧∧

14. The educator holds the jingle stick with her right hand and speaks to it. Then she moves it forward a little in the jingle bell rhythm, always at the same height. At the second line, at *shinga* she shakes the jingle stick back and forth in a lively way without special emphasis. (After a small break, both lines may be repeated.)

15. *Jingle sticks now:*
   Bing-bing-bing-bing.

   Bing - bing - bing - bing

   Binga-binga-binga-bing.
   ∧∧∧∧∧∧∧∧∧∧∧∧∧∧∧∧∧∧∧∧∧∧∧

15. The educator holds the jingle stick quiet again and speaks to it. Then she holds the stick nearer to her right ear and moves it forward with considerably smaller movements. She speaks the text quietly. The second line is performed as in 15, only more softly. (It could be repeated after a small pause.)

16. *Sound fine and clear for the baby dear...*

fine	and
clear	for
baby	dear

16. Now she holds the jingle stick horizontally in front of herself and swings it to and fro in the speech stress (as shown). This creates three small figures of eight. This could be repeated after a small pause.

17. *Shing-shing-shing-shing.*
   Shinga-shinga-shinga-shing.

17. The educator lifts the stick up again and plays with it, as shown in 14.

18. *Bing-bing-bing-bing.*
   Binga-binga-binga-bing!

18. She holds the stick closer to her right ear and plays with it, as shown in 15.

19. *Shinga-shinga-shinga-shinga*
/\/\/\/\/\/\/\/\/\/\/\/\/\/\/\/\/\/\

   shinga-shinga-shinga-shing!
/\/\/\/\/\/\/\/\/\/\/\/\/\/\/\/\/\

19. Now she shakes the jingle stick to and fro without special stress.

20. *All the jingles quiet keep*
   for the baby wants to sleep...

20. The educator covers the jingles with her left hand and holds the stick to her right ear. She listens until the metal balls inside the jingles stop rolling. The she rests the stick against her chest. Only then does she say *All the jingles quiet keep, for the baby wants to sleep.*

21. (Spoken)
   Therefore I gather the jingle sticks all
   and put them in the basket small.

21. The educator fetches the basket (or baskets) and collects the jingle sticks, perhaps with a helper.

22. *With the cloth I cover them tight.*
   In the basket they'll sleep all night.

22. When all sticks are in the basket she covers them with a coloured cloth while speaking the text. Then she puts the basket in its place.

23. *Mary and Joseph say:*
   "Thank you!

23. See Core Play, p. 47.

24. *For the 'shinga-shinga!' Thank you!"*

24. At *shinga-shinga* the educator shakes an imaginary jingle stick and bows again for *thank you!*

25. *And the baby smiles so dear, with the smiles so dear,*
   that their hearts turn warm with cheer,
   warm with cheer!

25. See Core Play, p. 47.

Continue with the Core Play section 5, or
Supplementary Scene *Call of the animals.*

5. KNOCK-KNOCK STICKS

This Supplementary Scene is particularly useful for a group with many prospective first graders or many boys. It may be inserted after the *It-is-enough song* or after *Sound of the silver cymbals*. *Call of the animals* should always follow it as a calming transition to the short version: *Angels guard the child* (p. 52). The game is played on the floor or sitting on stools.

The shepherds also had a thought
And for the dear Jesus child
their small wood sticks have brought.

Wood sticks – wood sticks:
knock-knock-knock-knock
knock-knock-knock-knock
knock-knock-knock-knock!
Wood sticks – wood sticks:
knock-knock-knock-knock
knock-knock-knock-knock
knock-knock-knock-knock!

Not too loud! Not too tough!
for baby Jesus
soft enough – soft enough!
Knock-knock-knock!
Knock-knock-knock!

The shepherds pack up their wood sticks all
and put them in the basket small.

Mary and Joseph say:
"Thank you!
For the 'knock-knock-knock!' Thank you!"
And the baby smiles so dear, smiles so dear,
that their hearts turn warm with cheer,
warm with cheer!

Note on wood sticks:
Prepare the sticks from soft wood or use simple branches from the forest (not hard wood), ready for knocking, so that speech and movement go together. Use the 'jingle sticks' method to distribute the wood sticks. Each child gets two sticks (one pair).

1. Wood sticks – wood sticks:

2. *Knock-knock-knock-knock*

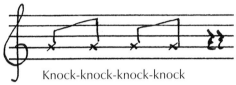

Knock-knock-knock-knock

Knock-knock-knock-knock
Knock-knock-knock-knock!

Knock - knock - knock - knock

3. *Wood sticks – wood sticks:*

4. *Knock-knock...etc.*

5. *Not too loud!*

6. *Not too tough!*

7. *for baby Jesus...*

1. The educator lifts both her right and left hand together, holding a stick in each, as if she wants to show them to the Jesus child. She speaks the words *wood sticks – wood sticks*.

2. She lowers the sticks and knocks them against each other, lightly, in speech rhythm.

3. As in direction 1 (see above).

4. As in direction 2 (see above).

5. The educator puts her hands (still holding the sticks) on her ears.

6. She holds the previous gesture and shakes her head to indicate 'no'.

7. She removes the sticks from her ears, reaching forward and pointing to the child in the manger.

8. *soft enough – soft enough!*

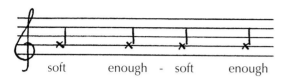

8. The educator knocks the right stick on the left stick very gently, in the direction of the child in the manger. Before each soft strike she makes a small upward circle with the stick.

9. *Knock-knock-knock!*
    Knock-knock-knock!

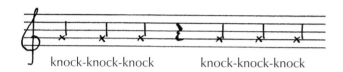

9. As in direction 8 (see above).The circles before the strike should be larger; this slows down the tempo. This should start a feeling of calm.

10. *The shepherds pack up their wood sticks all and put them in the basket small.*

10. Sticks are collected, as with the jingle sticks (see p. 76).

11. *Mary and Joseph say:*
    "Thank you!"'

11. See Core Play, p. 47.

12. *"For the 'knock-knock-knock-knock!'*
    Thank you!"

12. For the *knock-knock* the educator taps her stretched out fingers as if they were sticks.

13. *And the baby smiles so dear, smiles so dear,*
    that their hearts turn warm with cheer,
    warm with cheer!

13. See Core play, direction 8.

Continue the Core Play section 5, or continue
with *Call of the animals* (next section).

6. CALL OF THE ANIMALS

This game may be inserted after the *It-is-enough-song* in the Core Play or after the Supplementary Scenes with instruments. *Call of the animals* is rhythmic-musically formed. It is played kneeling on the floor. (When kneeling is too difficult, the whole game can be played sitting on stools.)

The animals too would bring joy to all.
So for the child
they sound their call.

The ox calls:

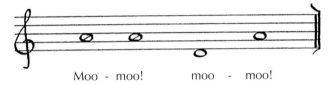

Moo - moo!   moo - moo!

The donkey calls:

Hee - haw!   Hee - haw!

The sheep call:

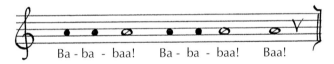

Ba - ba - baa!   Ba - ba - baa!   Baa!

Then quiet they keep all
and look upon the child
who shares their stall.
Mary and Joseph say:
"Thank you!
For your calling! Thank you!"
And the baby smiles so dear, smiles so dear,
that their hearts turn warm with cheer,
warm with cheer!

1. *The animals too would bring joy to all...*

   (Silent movement)

1. Standing, the educator turns to the children. She shows a little bowl with each hand, which she moves down slightly as if giving a present to someone, nodding approvingly at the word *joy*. Then she silently kneels.

2. *So for the child...*

2. With both palms joined, she points to the child.

3. The educator mimes a megaphone with both hands at her mouth.

3. *they sound their call...*

4. She makes the gesture of the ox, putting her fists, thumbs down, at the side of her forehead.

4. *The ox calls:*

5. The educator calls *moo-moo* in the marked tone, stretching her head forwards a little.

5. *Moo-moo! Moo-moo!*

6. *The donkey calls:*
   Hee-haw! Hee-haw!

6. The educator now makes the donkey gesture: flat hands, palms to the audience, on both sides of the forehead. At *Hee...* she stretches her upper body lightly. If possible she sings the marked note. If she has trouble reaching the high E, she should sing the fifth: A–D.

7. *The sheep call:*
   Ba-ba-baa! Ba-ba-baa! Baa!

(Silent movement)

7. Now the educator lays her crossed arms on her chest, hands hanging loosely in the paw position. She calls the *ba-ba-baa!* on the marked note. At each [^] she nods slightly. Then she sits down silently on her heels.

8. *Then quiet they keep all*
   and look upon the child
   who shares their stall.

8. The educator rests her hands flat on her thighs. At *and look upon the child* she bends her upper body and her head lightly. She remains in this position for a short while, then sits up again. At the word *stall* she makes the gesture for a roof with her arms and hands (see Core Play).

9. *Mary and Joseph say:*
   "Thank you!

9. See the Core Play, p. 47.

10. *For the calling: Thank you!'*

10. The educator makes a megaphone with both hands before her mouth.

11. *And the baby smiles so dear, smiles so dear,*
    that their hearts turn warm with cheer,
    warm with cheer!

11. See the Core Play, p. 47.

Continue the Core Play section 5: *Angels Guard the Child.*

7. The Complete Closing:

The Shepherds Leave

All the shep-herds and their sheep go to the field in mea-sured tread. The

heaven - ly won - der they have met!

Yes, the ba - by smiles so dear, the ba - by smiles so dear,

that the heart turns warm with cheer! Cheer! Cheer!

The shepherds all now homeward tread.
The heavenly wonder they have met.
Sheep and lambkin, trip-trip-trong
with the shepherds come along.
Sheep and lambkin, trip-trip-trong
with the shepherds come along.
Back in the pasture with their sheep
shepherds all sit down to sleep.
The shepherd wipes his good sheep dear
all over his soft fleece with care.
Then the shepherds and their sheep
settle down and fall asleep.
Sheep and shepherds, they dream all
of the Christ Child in the stall.

CONCLUSION

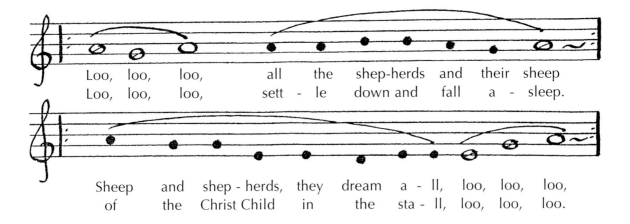

Loo, loo, loo,   all   the   shep-herds and their sheep
Loo, loo, loo,   sett - le down and   fall   a - sleep.

Sheep   and   shep - herds, they dream a - ll, loo, loo, loo,
of   the   Christ Child in   the sta - ll, loo, loo, loo.

In the stall, there sleep all
guarded by the angels bright
in the high, holy night,
in the Christmas night.

IT IS DONE

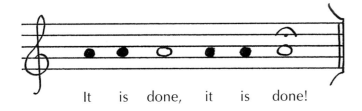

It   is   done,   it   is   done!

TREATS

At the end we have some treats.
Jesus each one fondly greets.
Open up! I'll give you one.
Chewing, chewing! Mmm – yum, yum!

The educator fetches the bowl with nuts or dried fruit. She walks from child to child and puts a sweet in each mouth (or into each hand). She repeats the text until everyone has a sweet.

CALL FOR CONCLUSION

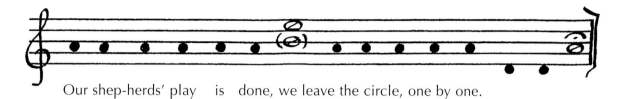

Our shep-herds' play   is   done, we leave the circle, one by one.

RETURN OF THE SHEPHERDS

All   the   shep-herds and their sheep go   to   the   field   in   mea-sured tread. The

heaven - ly   won - der they have met!

Yes, the   ba - by smiles so   dear,   the   ba - by smiles so   dear,

that   the   heart turns   warm   with   cheer!   Cheer!   Cheer!

1. *The shepherds all now homeward tread.*
   The heavenly wonder they have met...

1. The educator continues walking around the circle, right shoulder to the centre of the circle. Then she moves out of the play circle into the 'field' where she started in the beginning. She moves freely. Movement and speech rhythm need not coincide.

2. *Sheep and lambkin, trip-trip-trong*
   with the shepherds come along.
   Sheep and lambkin, trip-trip-trong
   with the shepherds come along...

2. With the sheep gesture she minces with light, small steps into the 'field'. After each step she pulls each knee up a bit. She does not match her steps to the beat.

Up the hill, down the hill may be inserted here.

3. *Back in the pasture with their sheep*
   shepherds all sit down to sleep....

3. The educator slows down and stands still. She waits until all the children stand too, then she sits down on her heels (or on a stool).

4. *The shepherd wipes his good sheep dear*
   all over his soft fleece with care...

4. She places her left arm diagonally across her chest pointing upward. With her right hand she strokes her left fist and arm lovingly. For each line of text, she strokes down slowly across fist and forearm.

5. *Then the shepherds and their sheep settle down and fall asleep. Sheep and shepherds, they dream all of the Christ Child in the stall.*

5. The educator bends her head and buries her face in her hands. She remains quiet in this gesture and begins to sing.

CONCLUSION

Loo, loo, loo,   all   the   shep-herds   and   their   sheep
Loo, loo, loo,   sett - le   down and   fall   a - sleep.

Sheep   and   shep - herds,   they   dream   a - ll,   loo,   loo,   loo,
of   the   Christ Child   in   the   sta - ll,   loo,   loo,   loo.

6. *Loo, loo, loo, all the shepherds and their sheep…*

6. She sings the conclusion softly, rocking to and fro in the swing of the melody with her face buried in her hands. If desired, she may hum a repeat or play the Choroi flute (see note on p. 15).

7. *In the stall, there sleep all…*

7. At the word *stall* the educator makes the stall roof with arms and hands and holds this gesture for a while. At *all* she rests her forehead lightly against her hands, still showing the roof. With this gesture she bends forward slightly and remains there for some time.

8. *Guarded by the angels bright…*

8. The educator rises silently and lifts her arms as wings.

9. *In the high, holy night,*
    (back) (forward) (back)
    in the Christmas night.

9. She lifts her arms a little higher and swings them back and forth. At *in the Christmas night* she lowers her arms into a blessing gesture, holding it and then slowly dissolving it.

IT IS DONE

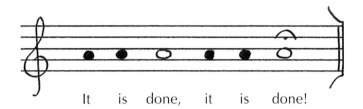

It   is   done,   it   is   done!

The educator strikes the cymbals gently before she sings, moving her arms to right and left and then back together. She sings *It is done!* into the dying cymbal tone twice.

TREATS

At the end there are some treats!
Christ Child each one fondly greets.
Open up! I'll give you one!
Chewing, chewing! Mmm – yum, yum!

The educator fetches the bowl with nuts or dried fruit. She walks from child to child and puts a sweet in each mouth (or into each hand). She repeats the text until everyone has a sweet.

CALL FOR CONCLUSION

Our shep-herds' play   is   done, we   leave the   cir - cle,   one   by   one.

The Three Kings Play

The Three Kings Play

Complete Three Kings Play

The complete Three Kings Play includes: Core Play, Supplementary Scenes, Journey to Egypt and Play Addition. It is important that the play can be performed without the various supplements and additions. The sequence of the core play is:

Procession – Arrival – Adoration – Offerings – Return accompanied by angel – Rocking and Conclusion

It aims to stress the story of the adoration of the 'royal son' in contrast to the events at the adoration of the heavenly child in the Shepherds Play. In order to deepen the experience, one can extend the core play bit by bit through the inclusion of Supplementary Scenes. (The Core Play with all the Supplementary Scenes is then the Complete Play.)

One starts with the Core Play for a time, then adds a Supplementary Scene, then another one. In this way, sections will be repeated continuously and new parts added. Younger children will not be overwhelmed, and new additions will keep older children interested.

At the conclusion, 'Journey to Egypt' will be added in a child-appropriate form, showing amazement without fear and sadness. This is the end either of the Core Play, when it is played alone, or the Complete Play with the Supplementary Scenes. It should be played at least three or four times. The Epiphany season extends to February 1 – one day before Candlemas.

Text in the Three Kings Play

An attempt has been made to form the text so it becomes musical by stressing rhythm and speech melody. The content is less prominent, so that the essence of the speech, the pulsing stream and sounding breath can be experienced. That speech is a movement-and-sound-action. The text is transformed into 'speech gestures' and physical gestures. Therefore the text can be experienced as a unified fulfilment of the gestures. Anything that would lead to abstract concepts has been avoided, for those cannot be shown in gesture and bearing, and cannot be made perceivable in a spatial, physical sense.

The play action

The Three Kings received the message of the birth of the royal child from the star. They had waited long for this prophesied moment. When the time was right, it appeared to them. They were 'wise magicians' and they received their revelation from cosmic worlds through a vision.

This happened in far-away lands, and they started on the long trek from the Empires of the East to Judea. The star then led them to Bethlehem, to the place where the child was to be found.

Gestures

The play revolves around the long journey and the star. The play space, where the procession moves along behind the star, is also included. The long journey becomes an experience.

> The angels hover in heaven's height
> the birds fly in airy space,
> the children walk to the Jesus child,
> they come to him from far away.

> The heavenly star, which led the wise
> men to the child, also shines in the
> eyes of the royal child.

> Then Jesus laughs, he thinks it right.
> And like two stars his eyes shine bright.

The star is also present in the 'crystal' as a six-pointed star. The six-star is the star of David. It is the symbol for the macrocosm. The star is hidden in the rose as the five-pointed star. It is the Pythagorean symbol of healing, and also the symbol for the human being. The child welcomes all who adore him in reverence and who bring him worthy offerings.

> Incense, myrrh and also gold
> angel bells with soft ding-dong,

Twitterbirdies' loving song –
rose that blooms in Christmas night –
crystal, shining like a star –
all this they bring from afar.
Joseph welcomes them within.
Gracefully does Mary bow
to all her gratitude does show.

It is a space illuminated by the light of reverence and the power of offering, a space penetrated by devotion, majesty and expanse.

After the priest kings had honoured their Lord, they were directed by a dream from the angel to return to their country by a different path. The star guided them to Bethlehem; then the angel led them quietly back to eastern lands.

In the scene 'Journey to Egypt', the long journey is the centre of the action once again. It is so far that Mary and the child cannot walk it. A little donkey carries them.

> And Joseph walks with measured tread.
> The angel with is wings outspread
> guides the holy family ahead
> walks unseen at their right hand
> to Egypt land.

The play circle

Small children are bound by sense perceptions. Therefore it is necessary that the Jesus child, the centre of the events, is physically perceptible – not as a naturalistic doll, but as a representation.

The throne with the child does not stand in the centre of the play circle, like the manger in the Shepherds Play. It is located in one of the two centres of a figure of eight.

In the beginning the royal child is covered by a cloth. When flying (as angels and birds), one follows the circle perimeter around the star. The star can also be put in the centre of the figure of eight, with the throne in front of it. Either way, the educator stands or sits next to the throne and attempts to return to this position after each large movement. The children sit inside the circle, not exactly on the perimeter – they could also sit in front or behind it.

Play Suggestions

Speech must be formed so that gesture and sound can be experienced rhythmically and musically.

Gestures must be prepared well before speaking so that speech always coincides with gesture. For all transitions into a different direction, or into different gestures, one must allow plenty of time. What is important is not the finished gesture or the end of the movement but actual creation of the movement.

For all gestures and movements it is important to have enough room for the movements so that the children don't bump into each other. If necessary, movements can be reduced in size.

The Three Kings Play: Overview

Preparation

- Building the play circle (set up star and star holder and stools, if used)
- Preparing the Kingly Jesus Child (covered at first)
- Preparing the basket for the bells
- Preparing the Choroi children's harp
- Getting the treats ready
- Dressing children in tabards, if using

The Core Play

A. STAR PROCESSION

1. Arrival
2. Adoration
3. Offerings (Supplementary Scenes 1–4)
4. Return
5. Rocking

B. IT IS DONE

C. TREATS

Supplementary Scenes *

1. *Angels*
2. *Birds*
3. *Children*
4. *Mutual devotion*
5. *Rest under the palm tree*

D. JOURNEY TO EGYPT

1. Prelude
2. Main play
3. Conclusion

PLAY ADDITION

The holy family rests

* The Supplementary Scenes 1, 2 and 3 may be played according to your choice. The fourth Supplementary Scene, Mutual devotion, is only fitting after the three preceding Supplementary Scenes. The play sequence without the Supplementary Scenes is the Core Play. The fifth Supplementary Scene may be added at any time.

The Three Kings Play (Core Play)

A. PROCESSIONAL SONG 1: STAR PROCESSION

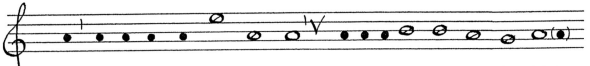

1. To - day, to - day is Three Kings Day! This is a great and won - der - ful day!
2. From far a - way come Three Kings strong. We, the chil - dren come a-long.
3. The wise men from the East so far bring o - ffer - ings with joy.

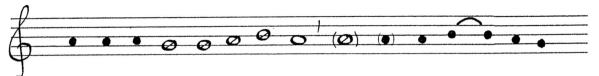

1. It is a day I like! Hu-rray! They are com-ing with the
2. We all all all come a - long. We like to fo-llow
3. O - ffer - ings for the Je - sus boy. They fo - llow their

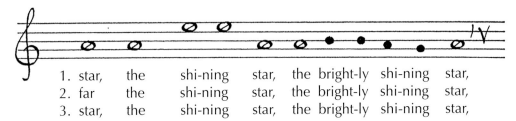

1. star, the shi-ning star, the bright-ly shi-ning star,
2. far the shi-ning star, the bright-ly shi-ning star,
3. star, the shi-ning star, the bright-ly shi-ning star,

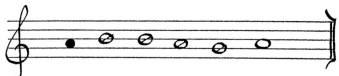

1. the bright and shi - ning star.
2. the bright and shi - ning star.
3. the bright and shi - ning star.

A. PROCESSIONAL SONG 2: THREE WISE MEN FOLLOW THE SHINING STAR

Three wise men fo - llow the shi-ning star,

With it they're com - ing from a - far to

See the child in Beth - le - hem that the

Star to them has shown that he should here be born. Three

wise men fo - llow the shi-ning star,

With it they're com - ing from a - far to

See the child in Beth - le - hem the

New - born heaven - ly king!

Directions for the processional song(s)

Only one of the processional songs should be sung. The educator takes the staff with the golden six-pointed (or eight-pointed) star, and lifts it up, showing it to the right, the left, and the middle, and sings three times:

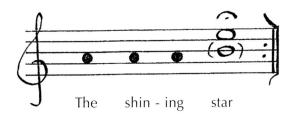

The shin-ing star

Then the educator begins the procession with the children following. It is good for an adult to carry the star, so that the procession moves through the rooms in an orderly way. This also prevents problems when the group is so large that not every child can have a turn carrying the star during the play.

The procession approaches the play area, then moves around it, establishing the play circle. When the circle has been formed, the star carrier continues a few more steps. She lifts the staff with the star, looking up at it. Now the play begins with the words *The star to Bethl'hem leads the way...*

(As an approach to the Epiphany season, one can end the play after the procession.)

1. ARRIVAL

The star to Beth'lem leads the way,
above the house to stop and stay.
Shines so bright!
The kings travel no more that night.

In this house they will abide.
Joseph welcomes them within:
"Come in! Come in!"
The kings now enter here,
find within the child so dear.

2. ADORATION

The wise men bend their knees low,
and their heads they bow so.
With devotion they honour the boy.
That they are with him
fills their hearts with joy.
They were guided by the bright star.
Christ, their Lord, they found from afar!

3. OFFERINGS

Bring offerings with joy:
gold,
frankincense,
and myrrh
they give to the little boy.
Mary says: "Thank you! Thank you!"
Then Jesus laughs, he thinks it right,
and like two stars his eyes shine bright!

4. RETURN

Caspar, Melchior, Balthasar,
the three holy kings
bow down in farewell.
With thankful hearts, with joyful hearts
they back to Eastern lands depart.
With thankful hearts, with joyful hearts
very quietly to their home depart.
The angel with his wings outspread,
guides the three wise kings ahead,
walks unseen to guide their band

back, back to Eastern land.
Guides, guides
guides them to Eastern land.
The kings homeward set their pace.
The adoration has taken place.

5. ROCKING

So tired was the little child.
Mary sings and rocks him mild.

1. shoom-shoom-shy, shoom-shoom-shy,　shoom-shoom-shy, shoom-shoom-shy!　I
2. shoom-shoom-shy, shoom-shoom-shy,　shoom-shoom-shy, shoom-shoom-shy!　I
3. shoom-shoom-shy, shoom-shoom-shy,　shoom-shoom-shy, shoom-shoom-shy!　I

1. call　I　call　that　sleep come nigh,　to　my　li - ttle　child so　dear,
2. sing　I　sing　that　dreams come nigh,　to　my　li - ttle　child so　dear,
3. pray　to　an - gels　to　come nigh,　to　my　li - ttle　child so　dear,

1. so　that　soon　he　slum - bers　here.
2. that　to　him　sweet　dreams　a - ppear.
3. so　that　he'll　be　guard - ed　here.

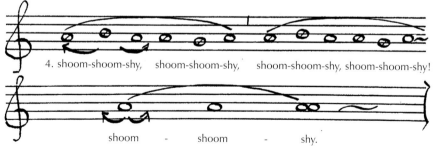

4. shoom-shoom-shy,　shoom-shoom-shy,　shoom-shoom-shy, shoom-shoom-shy!

shoom - shoom - shy.

Then the child's eyes are closing tight.
In mother's arms he sleeps all night.

B. It is done

Quiet into the house has come.
The Three Kings Play is done.

It   is   done,   it   is   done!

C. Treats

At the end there are some treats!
Christ Child each one fondly greets.
Open up! I'll give you one!
Chewing, chewing! Mmm – yum, yum!

The Three Kings Play   is   done! Time for eve-ry-one to   go   home.

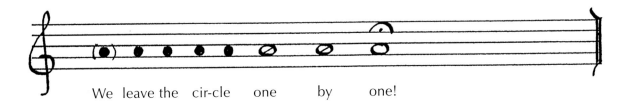

We leave the cir-cle   one   by   one!

The Three Kings Play: Directions

1. ARRIVAL

Text	**Movements**
1. *The star to Bethl'hem leads the way…*	1. The star carrier (educator) arrives behind the Jesus Child.
2. *Above the house…*	2. She turns towards the centre of the circle, lifting the star up.
3. *to stop and stay…*	3. The educator walks to the 'star stand' with the star staff. At *stay*, she places it in the stand.
4. *Shines so bright!*	4. The educator silently steps back into the circle, pointing with her right hand to the star in the stand.
5. *The kings travel no more that night…*	5. She lowers her right hand and turns her face to the circle centre. Then she shakes her head.
6. *In this house they will abide…*	6. The educator joins her fingertips above her head to form a roof.

7. *Joseph welcomes them within...*

7. The educator rests her hands lightly on her chest. Then she opens her arms in welcome (but not too wide). Then she makes a small bow.

8. *"Come in! Come in!"*

8. She gestures twice in a large arc, as if to welcome someone in.

9. *The kings now enter here...*

9. The educator stands straight in a majestic manner. She places her hands on her head above her temples with slightly spread fingers to form a crown. Then she takes two careful steps toward the child. She stops for a moment, then releases the 'crown' and uncovers the baby Jesus (who had been covered until then).

10. *find within the child so dear...*

10. She points to the child with both hands, palms facing each other, but not touching.

2. Adoration

1. *The wise men bend their knees low…*

2. *and their heads they bow so…*

3. *With devotion they honour the boy…*

4. *That they are with him…*

5. *fills their hearts with joy…*

6. *They were guided…*

7. *by the bright star…*

8. *Christ their Lord, they found…*

9. *from afar…*

1. The educator assumes the knee stand (or step stand): left knee on the floor, right foot planted on the floor in front of the left knee (about one step away). Her upper body is upright.

2. In the knee (or step) stand, she bends her head while her arms and hands hang loosely by her sides.

3. The educator continues in the gesture above as she speaks the words *With devotion…*

4. She crosses her lower arms across her chest, looking at the child and nodding at *him*.

5. She continues the previous gesture, but straightens her upper body.

6. The educator slowly lifts her hands toward the star.

7. She points directly to the star.

8. She lowers her hands and points again to the child, palms facing towards one another.

9. She makes a light bow, still in gesture 8. Her arms and hands are still stretched out toward the child, but she brings them in towards her own body a touch.

3. Offerings

1. *Bring offerings with joy:*

2. *gold...*

3. *frankincense...* (silent)

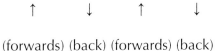

(forwards) (back) (forwards) (back)

1. The educator turns her hands, palms up, so that they become two small bowls next to each other. At *offerings*, she shows the bowls to the child.

2. The educator assumes the knee stand (or sits down on a stool) and joins her hands at the little fingers to make *one* bowl. In this bowl lies the imagined gold that is shown to the child. She holds this gesture for a while.

3. The educator holds her hands upright, fingertips touching, and the balls of her hands touching. There is a hollow space between her two hands, and gaps between her fingers so smoke could escape out of the cracks of this vessel. She quietly swings her hands in the given rhythm.

4. *and myrrh…*

4. Now she forms a 'box with lid' with her hands. With her left hand, she forms a small bowl again, well rounded. Her right hand is also a bowl, with the back of her hand facing up. She covers her left hand with her right hand as a 'lid', so the ball of her right hand lies on the fingertips of her left hand. She allows time to form this gesture.

5. *they give to the little boy…*

5. The educator again holds her hands as two small bowls. She points with the two bowls to the child and bows, remaining there a short time. Then she straightens herself silently.

6. *Mary says: "Thank you!"*

6. She makes the symbolic gesture for Mary: while sitting on her heels, she crosses her lower arms in front of her chest, without her arms touching. She bows in this Mary gesture.

7. *"Thank you!"*

7. Keeping the gesture for Mary, the educator straightens and then bows once more.

8. *Then Jesus laughs, he thinks it right…*

Then Jesus laughs, he thinks it right…

8. The educator claps in a light rhythm, as shown on the left. After each clap, she makes a small loop upward.

9. *and like two stars his eyes shine bright…*

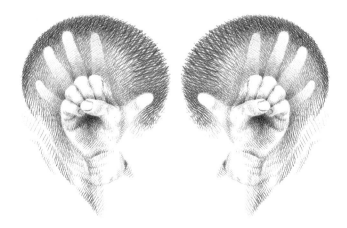

9. The educator spreads her hands and fingers, palms forward, at eye-height, moving her hands slightly forward. At *shine* she draws in her fingers and moves her hands back a little. At *bright* she spreads her fingers again. This should represent glittering and blinking.

Supplementary Scenes 1–3 may be inserted in any preferred selection. Supplementary Scene 4 is only suitable if Supplementary Scenes 1–3 have all been played.

4. RETURN

1. (Silent movement)

2. *Caspar, Melchior, Balthasar…*

3. *the three holy kings…*

4. *bow down in farewell…*

5. *With thankful hearts, with joyful hearts…*

6. (Silent movement)

7. *they back to Eastern lands depart.*
   With thankful hearts, with joyful hearts
   very quietly to their home depart…

---

1. The educator slowly straightens and stands up. (This is unnecessary if following *Mutual devotion* as she would be standing already.)

2. As she speaks the names of the kings, she turns first to the left, then forward, then finally to the right, bowing lightly each time (primarily with her head).

3. The educator places the crown on her head.

4. She lowers her arms to a hanging position and bows.

5. The educator straightens and crosses her arms across her chest. In this position, she nods once more at the word *joyful*.

6. Keeping the gesture from 5, the educator makes a quarter turn so her right shoulder points to the circle centre.

7. She now walks clockwise around the circle in quiet steps with children following. It is not necessary that the children go one behind the other, they may move next to each other. The speech and the steps need not always coincide. (It may happen occasionally but there is no real need for it.)

8. *The Angel with his wings outspread*
   guides the three wise kings ahead,
   (forwards)   (back)
   walks unseen to guide their band
   (forwards)   (back)
   back, back to Eastern land.
   (forwards)   (back)
   Guides… (silent movement)
   (forwards)   (back)
   guides… (silent movement)
   (forwards)   (back)
   guides them back to eastern land.
   (forwards) (back)   (forwards)   (back)

8. The educator lifts her arms as wings and continues around the circle with light, gliding steps while moving her wings forwards and back in the rhythm noted to the left. She speaks the last line very slowly, so that the wing movements always stay in the same rhythm. After the words *eastern land*, the educator comes to a stop. Only after everyone is standing still does she turn her face to the centre.

9. *The kings homeward set their pace…*

9. Making a high arc to the left with both hands, the educator shows the distance the wise men still must travel.

10. *The adoration has taken place.*

10. As an end to the play, the educator bows again before the royal child, palms facing each other, in a prayer gesture. (Her hands do not touch.)

The holy three kings rest under the palm tree may be inserted here.

5. ROCKING

1. *So tired was the little child…*

2. (Silent movement)

3. *Mary sings…*

4. *and rocks him mild…*

1. The educator sits back on her heels or sits down again on a stool.

2. She bends her head without speaking, and rests her face in both hands. She remains in this gesture for a while.

3. She lifts her head and puts her hands in her lap. She sounds the note A. Then she lays her arms together. Her hands grasp her forearms.

4. The educator rocks the imaginary child in her arms.

5. *Shoom-shoom-shy, shoom-shoom-shy*
   Shoom-shoom etc.

5. She still holds the imaginary child in her arms (see illustration on p. 111) and rocks him to and fro.

6. *...I* <u>*call*</u>*, I call*
   that <u>*sleep*</u> *come nigh,*
   <u>*to*</u> *my little* <u>*child*</u> *so dear*

6. At the underlined words the educator beckons as if to welcome sleep. Her movements are slow and quiet.

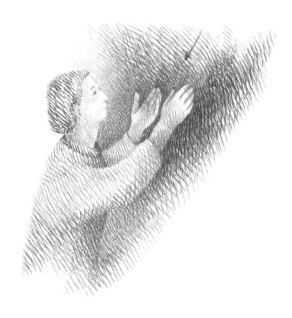

7. *so that soon he slumbers here...*

7. She bends her head and rests her left cheek on her hands, palms together.

8. *Shoom-shoom-shy etc...*

8. Rocking, as described in 5.

9. *...I sing, I sing*
    that dreams come nigh...

9. The educator lifts her hands up, palms turned to each other, just above her head. At *that dreams come nigh* she bends her hands back to form a large bowl.

10. <u>to</u> *my little* <u>child</u> *so dear...*

10. At *to* and *child* she gestures lightly towards his head. These are small movements.

11. *that to him sweet dreams appear…*

11. The educator places her hands on her cheeks. Her thumbs touch her ears. She lowers her lids, without fully closing her eyes. She stays in this gesture for a little while.

12. *Shoom-shoom-shy etc…*

12. She rocks as described on p. 111.

13. *I pray to angels to come nigh…*

13. The educator starts in the prayer gesture: hands, palms together, held before her chest. Now she raises her hands in a flowing movement. By *angels* her wrists are above her head. Without stopping, she opens her hands, palms to the audience, and moves her arms apart to right and left to form two wings (angel gesture). See illustration.

14. *to my little child so dear…* (forwards) (back)	14. She moves her 'wings' (and her upper body, lightly) slowly, to make light wing strokes forwards and back.
15. *so that he be guarded here…*	15. Now the educator turns her palms down and lowers her arms to the height of her waist. She holds them there a while in a gesture of blessing and shelter.

16. *Shoom-shoom-shy…* *Shoomm-shoomm-shy…*	16. The educator resumes rocking, as before.
17. *Shoom-shoom-shy…* 	17. The educator sings the last *shoom-shoom-shy* very softly and slowly. She brings her arms closer to her body, still in the rocking position. She is now rocking in a barely visible movement forwards, back and forwards again (see the arrows under the words).
18. *Then the child's eyes are closing tight.* *In mother's arms he sleeps all night…*	18. The educator looks down on the imaginary child in her arms and speaks the final words softly.

B. IT IS DONE

1. (Silent movement)

2. *Quiet...*

3. *into the house has come...*

4. (Silent movement)

1. The educator rises to a knee stand. (If she sat on a stool for *shoom-shoom-shy*, she remains seated.) She places her right hand at her right ear and listens for a while.

2. At *quiet* she still holds her hand to her ear.

3. At *into the house* the educator's fingertips meet just above her head, to show a roof.

4. Now she stands up.

5. *The Three Kings Play...*

6. *is done...*

7. *It is done...*

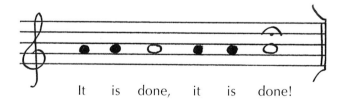

It   is   done,   it   is   done!

5. She forms a crown on her head with her hands and remains standing with the crown for a little while.

6. The educator takes her hands down and spreads her arms as if to say 'It's all gone.'

7. Before singing, the educator strikes the cymbals very gently, then moves her arms apart to right and left and then back again. She sings the A into the fading tone: *It is done!* This is repeated.

C. TREATS

At the end there are some treats!
Christ Child each one fondly greets.
Open up! I'll give you one!
Chewing, chewing! Mmm – yum, yum!

The educator takes the bowl with apple slices, prunes, figs, raisins or hazelnuts and distributes them to the children while speaking the verse. She continues until all have received a treat. If the group is large, an assistant may help with the distribution, so that the children will not have to wait too long for their treat.

The Three Ki - ngs Play is done! Time for ev-ery-one to go home.

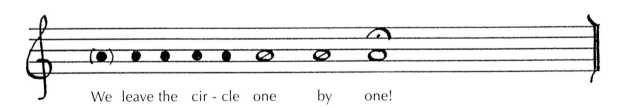

We leave the cir - cle one by one!

Note: Physical well-being fills the children when the play reaches all the way to their digestion! Give them plenty of time for chewing. Then the play action dissolves with the Call for conclusion and with clean-up. If using tabards, taking them off returns the children to everyday activity.

Supplementary Scenes

1. ANGELS

Have your heard it tell
who came along as well?
The angels, yes, the angels.
They also would be with the child!
Gliding from the heavens high
down upon the earth they fly,
glide into the dwelling here
come to visit Jesus dear.

Joseph welcomes them within:
"Come in! Come in!"

Small bells of golden hue
they bring along now, too,
playing softly: ding – dong,
an angel song.

Ding-ding-ding-ding!
Dingalingalingaling!
Ding-ding-ding-ding!
Dingalingalingaling!
Dingalingalingaling
dingalingalingaling!
Ding! – ding! – ding!

The angels stop their little bells' ring
that for a while we cannot (not at all)
hear them ding.

They play softly again: ding – dong
for the Christ child their song.

Ding-ding-ding-ding!
Dingalingalingaling!
Ding-ding-ding-ding!
Dingalingalingaling!
Dingalingalingaling
dingalingalingaling!
Ding! – ding! – ding!

All the bells must quiet keep,
for the child now wants to sleep.

Mary says: "Thank you!
You bright angels! Thank you!"

Then Jesus laughs, he thinks it right;
and like two stars his eyes shine bright.

1. *Have you heard it tell*
   who came along as well?

2. (Silent movement)

3. *The angels, yes, the angels...*

4. *they also would be with the child!*
   (forward) (back)

5. *Gliding from the heavens high*
   (forward)   (back)
   gently down to earth they fly,
   (forward)   (back)
   glide into the dwelling here...
   (forward)   (back)
   (Gliding... gliding...)
   (forward)   (back)

1. The educator, still kneeling (or sitting on a stool) turns to the children and asks: *Have you heard...*

2. She gets up, lifting her arms, palms forward, in the wing gesture.

3. After she has formed the gesture above, she says *The angels...*

4. She accompanies the words with a light 'wing stroke' forwards and back.

5. Now the educator, still holding the wing gesture, makes a quarter turn (right shoulder to the circle enter). Then she flies clockwise. The children may 'fly along' too. As she glides, walking and speaking, she moves her 'wings' forwards and back as noted. In order to return to the starting position, the word 'gliding' and the accompanying wing movements may be repeated several times (depending on the available space and the number of children present).

6. *come to visit Jesus dear…*	6. The educator gradually comes to a stop with a quarter turn, so she is facing centre. Her 'wings' remain slightly lifted.
7. *Joseph welcomes them within…*	7. She puts her hands on her chest. Then she spreads her arms in welcome, but not too wide. She makes a small bow.

8. *"Come in! Come in!"*	8. The educator beckons in a big arc, as if she wanted to call someone towards her. She does this twice.
9. (Silent movement)	9. She lowers her arms. She gets the covered basket containing the bells on a ring. She holds it up to everyone and shakes it a bit. All listen to the fine ringing. Then the educator removes the cloth.
10. *Small bells of golden hue…*	10. At *small bells* the educator grasps the ring, and takes it out of the basket, lifting it up for all to see.

11. *they bring along now, too…*

12. (Silent movement)
∧∧∧∧∧∧∧∧∧∧∧∧∧∧∧∧∧

13. *playing softly: ding – dong…*

14. (Silent movement)
∧∧∧∧∧∧∧∧∧∧∧∧∧∧∧∧∧

15. *an angel song…*

16. *I pass the little bells about.*
for each one I take one out.

17. For (name of child)… for…

11. She moves it in an arc from left to right and shows it to the children.

12. Now she holds the little bell about head height and shakes it lightly.

13. After the bells sound has died down, she speaks: *playing softly…*

14. She rings the little bell again, softly and delicately.

15. After the sound of the little bell has died away, the educator says *an angel song.*

16. She shakes the basket once more and then speaks the words: *I pass…*

17. As she speaks, the educator rounds the circle clockwise and hands out the little bells. (Depending on the occasion she may encourage the children by adding the children's names.)

Note: The handing out of bells is incorporated into the play so as to avoid interruption to the play action. If there are more than fifteen children it is advisable that a second person distributes bells from a second basket. See instructions for handing out the jingle sticks, (p. 76). When every child has a little bell and the baskets are put aside, the play begins. Of course, the children were already playing with their bells as they were handed out, so quiet has to be established before the bell game can begin.

18. (Silent movement)

18. The educator holds her little bell about head height and shakes it loudly, so that all the children notice it.

19. *The angels stop their little bells' ring...*

19. She encloses the little bell with her free hand, to demonstrate stopping.

20. (Silent movement)

20. Then she holds the (now hidden) little bell to her right ear and listens.

21. *that for a while one cannot (not at all) hear them ding...*

21. She holds the bell very quietly to her ear and speaks the words. At *not at all* she shakes her head.

PLAY WITH THE LITTLE BELLS

1. *For the Christ child...*

2. *their song...*

3. *Ding-ding-ding-ding!*
   •   •   •   •

4. *Dingalingalinglingaling!*
   ∧∧∧∧∧∧∧∧∧∧∧∧∧∧∧

5. *Ding-ding-ding-ding!*
   •   •   •   •

6. *Dingalingalinglingaling!*
   ∧∧∧∧∧∧∧∧∧∧∧∧∧

7. *Dingalingalinglingaling dingalingaling!*
   ∧∧∧∧∧∧∧∧∧∧∧∧∧ ∧∧∧∧∧∧∧∧

1. The educator moves her right hand toward the child while holding the little bell by its ring. For a while she holds the little bell near the child.

2. Now she draws the little bell closer to herself.

3. With her left index finger, she taps the dangling bell. With each tap of the little bell the educator says *Ding*. (She could raise the little bell and lower it again after each tap and then tap anew.)

4. As she speaks the *dingalingalinglingaling* she shakes the little bell lightly towards the child. Then she brings it closer again to herself for more taps.

5. As above (see 3).

6. As above (see 4).

7. As above (see 4). After the last *ling* she takes the little bell back for new tapping.

8. Ding! – ding – ding!
    •   •   •

8. Now there is more time between each tap. If needed, the educator may lift the little bell somewhat higher after the tapping. (The children should be allowed to use their other fingers for tapping.)

9. *The angels stop their little bells' ring…*

9. The educator encloses the dangling little bell with her left hand.

10. (Silent movement)

10. She hold the little bell to her ear and listens.

11. *that for a while we cannot…*

11. The educator holds the little bell very quietly to her ear and speaks the words very softly.

12. *not at all… hear them ring…*

12. She listens again and shakes her head.

13. *They play softly again…*

13. The educator takes her hand from the little bell. She moves it forward towards the child. By *their song* she returns the bell to its original position.

14. *Ding-ding-ding-ding … etc.*
    •   •   •   •

14. She now repeats the play sequence from 3 to 8 (see above).

15. *All the bells must quiet keep…*

15. The educator covers the bell with her left hand…

16. *for the child now wants to sleep…*

16. She rests both hands with the enclosed bell on her chest.

17. *Therefore I gather the little bells all and put them in the basket small.*

17. The educator gets the basket and goes round gathering the little bells. (If there are more than fifteen children, see the note on p. 76.)

18. *With the cloth I cover them tight. In the basket they'll sleep all night.*

18. She covers the basket(s) with the cloth and puts it (or them) away.

19. *Mary says: "Thank you!"*

19. The educator lowers herself on to her heels, crossing her forearms across her chest. Her arms do not touch her chest. She bows at *thank you* in the Mary gesture.

20. *You bright angels: "Thank you!"*

20. Keeping the symbolic gesture for Mary, the educator straightens and then bows once more.

21. *Then Jesus laughs, he thinks it right...*

Then Jesus laughs, he thinks it right...

21. The educator claps in a light rhythm as shown on the left. After each clap she makes a small loop upward.

22. *and like two stars his eyes shine bright.*

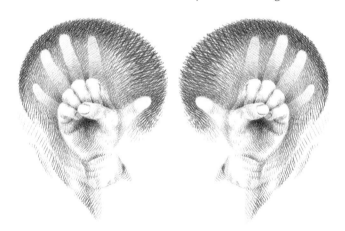

22. The educator spreads her hands and fingers, palms forward, at eye-height, moving her hands slightly forward. At *shine* she draws in her fingers and moves her hands back a little. At *bright* she spreads her fingers again. This should represent glittering and blinking.

At this point, one may add the Conclusion (as in the Core Play),
Return, Rocking, It is done, or one can insert a further Supplementary Scene.

2. THE BIRDIES

Have you heard it tell,
who came along as well?
The birdies, yes, the birdies.
They also would be with the child.
When they came, those wise men strong,
all the birdies flew along.

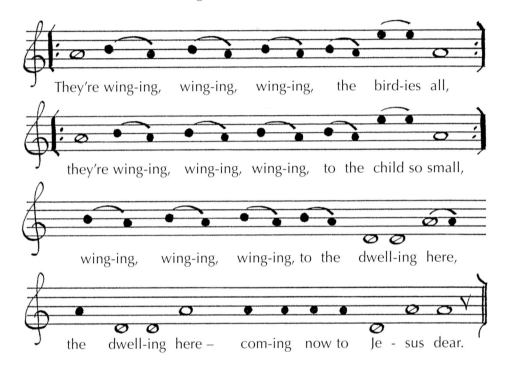

They're wing-ing, wing-ing, wing-ing, the bird-ies all,
they're wing-ing, wing-ing, wing-ing, to the child so small,
wing-ing, wing-ing, wing-ing, to the dwell-ing here,
the dwell-ing here – com-ing now to Je - sus dear.

Joseph welcomes them within:
"Come in, come in!"
They sit by the child, twitter softly:
Tewitt – tewitt – cheep – cheer.
Tewitt – tewitt – cheep – cheer.
Jesus small, you are my dear!
Tewitt – tewitt – cheep – cheer.
Tewitt – tewitt – cheep – cheer.

Mary says: "Thank you! Thank you!"
Then Jesus laughs, he thinks it right;
and like two stars his eyes shine bright.

1. *Have you heard it tell,* *who came along as well?*	1. The educator turns to the children sitting on their heels on the floor or standing in a loose circle after the previous scene. She addresses the children.
2. *The birdies, yes the birdies…* 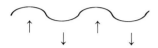	2. She lifts her arms in a light flying movement and speaks almost in a sing-song. The wing strokes follow the words as shown on the left.
3. *They also would be with the child…*	3. With both hands, palms up, the educator points to the child on the throne.
4. *When they came…*	4. She makes a movement with both hands, as if to wave something towards herself.
5. *those wise men strong…*	5. The educator stands up straight. She places her hands on her head above her temples, fingers slightly spread and lightly bent, to represent a crown.

6. *all the birdies flew along…*

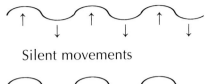

Silent movements

6. The educator makes light flying movements from the elbow, her lower arms and hands swinging loosely along. With her right shoulder, she turns to the circle centre and 'flies' clockwise about the circle. The children follow in loose order.

7.

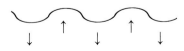

They're wing-ing, wing-ing, wing-ing, the bird-ies all,

they're wing-ing, wing-ing, wing-ing, to the child so small,

wing-ing, wing-ing, wing-ing, to the dwell-ing here,

the dwell-ing here – com-ing now to Je - sus dear.

7. The educator tunes to the A in preparation for singing. Children and educator sing the song as they 'fly' about. The children imitate the flying movements as well as they can. It is not necessary that the children fly in the right musical rhythm. The educator's wing beat must be in time with the song text.

They're winging, winging, winging,

the birdies all.

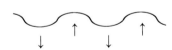

8. *They're winging, winging, winging…*

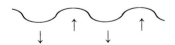

8. The wing beats of the educator should be rhythmical as shown in the melody. Her feet run freely, gliding. She should attempt to get back to her starting position.

9. *to the child so small…*

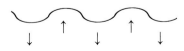

9. Continue 'flying' as shown. The *winging, winging* may be repeated as needed.

10. *Winging, winging, winging, to the…*

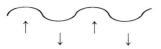

10. As before (see 8).

11. *dwelling here…*

11. The educator turns to the circle centre with one large wing stroke.

12. *the dwelling here…*

12. At the second *the dwelling here* she stands still and makes the shape of a roof.

13. *coming now to Jesus dear…*

13. The educator points to the child with both hands, palms up.

14. *Joseph welcomes them within:*

14. She puts her hands on her chest. Then she spreads out her arms in welcome, but not too wide. She makes a small bow.

15. *"Come in, come in!"*

15. The educator moves her hands towards her body as if she wanted to call someone to her. She does this twice.

16. (Silent movement preparation)

16. Change to the hand gesture for the birdie.

17. *They sit by the child…*

17. The educator holds her left index finger at chest height to form a small 'twig'. At the word *child* she leans her right wrist on it, hand formed in a loose fist. From her fist she stretches her thumb and right index finger so their fingertips touch. This may be done standing, in the knee stand, or sitting on a stool.

18. *twitter softly…*

18. The birdie makes a small bow to the child on the throne.

19. *Tewitt – tewitt – cheer*
    >   >   >

19. The educator opens and shuts the little beak as shown on text.

20. *Tewitt – tewitt – cheep – cheer*
    >   >   >

20. The size of the beak opening varies: at > she opens the beak wide, at > only a little.

21. *Jesus small, you are my dear…*
    > >   >   >

21. The educator sounds the call of the birdies in various tone heights. For example *Jesus small, you are…* called in a descending voice and *my dear* first high, then low.

22. *Tewitt – tewitt – cheep – cheer*
    >   >   >

22. The *tewitt – tewitt* could, for example, be called in the same tone, then the *cheep – cheer* first high, then low.

23. *Tewitt – tewitt – cheep – cheer*
    >   >   >

23. For the repetition, the speech melody could be varied.

24. *Mary says: "Thank you!"*

24. The educator lowers herself on to her heels, crossing her forearms across her chest. Her arms do not touch her chest. She bows in the Mary gesture.

25. *"Thank you!"*

25. Keeping the symbolic gesture for Mary, the educator straightens and then bows once more.

26. *Then Jesus laughs, he thinks it right…*

26. The educator claps in a light rhythm as before. After each clap she makes a small loop upward.

27. *and like two stars his eyes shine bright.*

27. The educator spreads her hands and fingers, palms forward, at eye-height, moving her hands slightly forward. At *shine* she draws in her fingers and moves her hands back a little. At *bright* she spreads her fingers again. This should represent glittering and blinking.

Note: If you decide to draw the play to a conclusion here, *Return, Rocking, It is done* should follow now.

3. THE CHILDREN

Have you heard tell
who came as well?
The children, yes, the children!

All the children, short and tall
would like to be with Jesus small.
When they came, the wise men strong,
all the children came along.
The children, the children,
they all came along.
The children, the children,
they all came near.
They wanted to see Jesus dear.

Joseph welcomes them within:
"Come in! Come in!"
They kneel before the boy
and bring their gifts with joy:
offer him the crystal bright
shining like a star at night.
They also bring to him a rose
That blooms in the holy night's repose.
The crystal
and a rose,
these fine gifts, with joy
they give to the Jesus boy.

Mary says: "Thank you!
Thank you!"
Then Jesus laughs, he thinks it right;
and like two stars his eyes shine bright.

1. *Have you heard tell* *who came as well?*	1. The educator turns to the children. The children will still be standing in a loose circle from the previous game. They sit on their heels or stools, or kneel in a knee stand.
2. *The children, yes, the children!*	2. She lays both hands flat on her body at stomach height and gives a small nod, while pointing to herself.
3. *All the children short and tall…*	3. The educator turns her hands and lays them on imaginary children's heads. At *short* she places her hand at waist height, at *tall*, just below her own head.
4. *would like to be with Jesus small…*	4. She points with both hands, palms up, to the child on the throne.
5. *When they came, the wise men strong…*	5. The educator puts her hands on her head above the temples, her fingers lightly spread to form a crown.

6. *All the children came along…*

6. Now she dissolves the crown gesture and makes a quarter turn, so that her right shoulder points to the circle centre. She starts to walk clockwise around the circle. The children follow her in no precise order.

7. *The children, the children,*
they all came along.
The children, the children,
they all came near…

7. The educator moves at a medium walking pace, speaking freely. Her speech and walking need not coincide. This prevents the movement from becoming a march. The educator should aim to return to her point of departure. The text may be repeated to allow time for this. Towards the end she lessens her walking speed to come to a stop.

8. *they wanted to see Jesus dear…*

8. She turns her face to the centre and points to the child with both hands.

9. *Joseph welcomes them within…*

9. She puts her hands on her chest. Then she spreads out her arms in welcome, but not too wide. She makes a small bow.

10. *"Come in! Come in!"*

10. The educator gestures as if to call someone towards her. She does this twice.

11. *They kneel before the boy…*

11. Slowly, the educator assumes the knee stand (on both knees).

12. *and bring their gifts with joy…*

12. She forms a bowl with her hands.

13. *offer him the crystal bright…*

13. She forms her hands into fists in front of her chest, pressing them together. This forms the 'crystal.'

14. *shining like a star at night…*

   a)   b)   c)   d)

   e) (Silent movement)

14. a) The educator opens her fists and spreads her fingers, still holding her hands at chest height, palms to the audience.

   b) She pushes her spread fingers forwards; left hand behind her right hand.

   c) At *star* she pushes the spread fingers of her left hand through the gaps of the spread fingers of her right hand. Her fingers and her thumbs, sticking out at the side, represent gleaming rays.

   d) The educator raises the star slowly straight up, just above her head, and lets it shine for a while.

   e) She lowers the star quietly.

15. *They also brought to him a rose…*

15. The educator covers her loosely formed left fist with her right hand to represent a flower.

16. *That blooms in the holy night's repose...*

16. The educator opens both hands slowly. She speaks the text slowly. Only at *holy night* has the blossom opened. The balls of her hands touch and her fingers are slightly bent.

17. *The crystal...*

17. The educator again shows the crystal as in 13. She silently repeats gestures in 14.

18. *and a rose...*

18. She forms the rose gesture once more (see 15), then silently repeats the opening of the bud (see 16), allowing herself plenty of time.

19. *these fine gifts, with joy...*

19. The educator forms a bowl with her hands (see 12).

20. *they give to the Jesus boy...*

20. She lowers the bowl to the floor while sitting back down on her heels.

21. Mary says: "Thank you!"

21. The educator lowers herself on to her heels, crossing her forearms across her chest. Her arms do not touch her chest. She bows in the Mary gesture.

22. *"Thank you!"*

22. Keeping the gesture for Mary, the educator straightens and then bows once more.

23. *Then Jesus laughs, he thinks it right...*

Then Jesus laughs, he thinks it right...

23. The educator claps in a light rhythm as shown. After each clap she makes a small loop upward.

24. *and like two stars his eyes shine bright...*

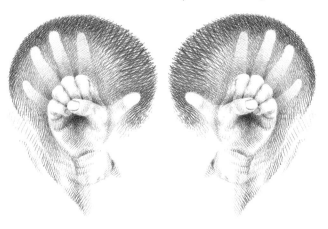

24. The educator spreads her hands and fingers, palms forward, at eye-height, moving her hands forwards slightly. At *shine* she draws in her fingers and moves her hands back a little. At *bright* she spreads her fingers again.

Note: If the first three Supplementary Scenes (*Angels*, *Birdies* and *Children*) were played, the Supplementary Scene *Mutual devotion* may now follow. Then the angels, the birdies and the children are gathered with the three kings in mutual devotion to the royal child. If only one or two of the first three Supplementary Scenes have been played, continue directly with *Return*, *Rocking*, and *It is done*.

4. Mutual devotion

The angels their wings hold,
the children their hands fold,
the birds their heads nod, nod,
the wise men kneel on the sod.

Thus in devotion mild
they honour the royal child,
to whom they have come today
with the bright star
from far away.

1. *The angels their wings hold....*

1. The educator stands up and raises her arms as wings. She holds this gesture for a moment.

2. *The children their hands fold...*

2. She joins her hands in front of her chest with her palms together crossing at the fingertips.

3. *The birds their heads nod, nod...*

3. She sets her right hand on top of her left. Her left index finder extends level from her fist. Then she inclines the bird's head each time at *nod* and returns it to its original position.

4. *The wise men kneel on the sod...*

4. The educator crosses her arms over her chest. She then sets her right foot a little forward at *kneel*. Keeping her arms crossed, she bends her knee a little and bows.

5. *Thus with devotion mild...*

5. She straightens up, pulling her foot back and planting it next to her left foot. Her arms remain crossed.

6. *they honour the royal child...*

6. With arms crossed on her chest, she bows deeply.

7. *to whom they have come today...*

7. As the educator slowly straightens, she releases her crossed arms from her chest. At *come* she lets them hang by her side, palms forward.

8. *with the bright star...*

8. She points with both hands to the star behind the throne. She holds it for a while.

9. *from far away...*

9. With raised hands, she points into the distance.

Now move on to *Return, Rocking* and *It is done*.

5. The three holy kings rest under the palm tree

Arrived in the Eastern lands
they all stop to rest.
The Holy Kings Three
under the palm tree,
under the palm tree stop to rest.
The angel guards their dream.
He takes his heavenly harp
and softly plays for the three
a dream melody.

Spoken: 'a dream melody'

Of what do they dream then?
They dream of Bethlehem,
of the place
from which they gratefully set their pace
back, back to Eastern lands.

In the house in Bethlehem
so tired was the little child.
Mary sings and rocks him mild.

This Supplementary Scene may be inserted at
the end of *Return* (the fourth part of the Core Play).

1. (Silent)

2. *Arrived in Eastern lands…*

3. *they all stop to rest…*

4. *The holy kings three…*

1. The educator comes to a standstill, arms still raised in the wing gesture. She waits until all the children have stopped too.

2. With both arms moving in a wide arc, she points with both hands to the left.

3. The educator dissolves the angel gesture, lowers her arms next to her body and, at the word *rest*, bends her head.

4. With both hands she shows a crown on her head.

5. *under the palm tree...*

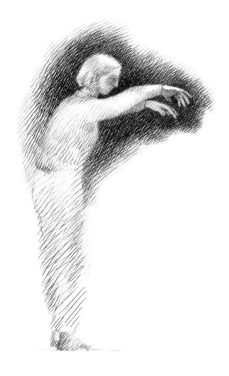

6. *under the palm tree stop to rest...*

7. *The angel guards their dream...*

5. The educator lifts her arms and hangs her hands down in front, as hanging palm leaves. To make it easier for the the children to copy, she should not make this gesture too high.

6. The educator swings her upper body forward a little and back, as if blown by a soft wind. Then she takes her arms down, and at the same time, lowers herself slowly into the knee stand. Her arms hang beside her body, and her head is slightly bent.

7. Still in the knee stand the educator lifts up her arms in the angel gesture. At *guards*, she moves the wings forward a little to form a sheltering gesture. She holds this gesture for a while. Now she sits down on her heels, and puts her hands against her cheek. At the word *dream* she snuggles her slightly raised face into her hands. She looks down. She holds this gesture for a while.

8. *He takes his heavenly harp…*

8. The educator picks up the Choroi children's harp. She sets herself in position to play; this can be sitting on her heels, or on a stool or chair. Then she strikes the A note gently.

9. *and softly plays for the three…*

9. She rests her slightly bent head on her right hand.

10. *a dream melody…*

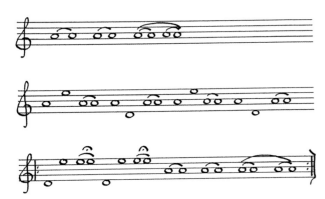

10. She plays the dream melody. After each tone she raises her hand, pointing into the air to draw attention to the note. Then she listens after the tone has been played. This way she makes the 'sound experience' perceivable for the children through physical gesture. After the last tone has died out, the educator puts the harp away, gently and quietly.

11. *Of what do they dream then?*

11. After the educator has put away the harp, she quietly makes again the dream gesture again: face turned upwards, eyes half-closed, snuggled into her hands. Sitting on her heels, she remains in this gesture for a while. Then, softly, she says the words: *Of what do they dream then?*

12. *They dream of Bethlehem…*

12. The educator remains in the dream gesture with lowered eyelids.

13. *of the place…*

13. She opens her eyes, rises into the knee stand and raises both arms in an upward arc.

14. *from which they gratefully set their pace...*

14. She joins her fingers above her head to form a roof.

15. *back, back to Eastern lands...*

15. She takes her hands down. Then she shows her empty hands as if to show that the house is really empty. At *back*, she brings her hands to the side of her head and then in a large arc forward, pointing far away.

16. *In the house in Bethlehem...*

16. At the word *house*, the educator shows again the roof with both hands.

17. *so tired was the little child...*

17. She now sits back on her heels or on a stool or chair. At *so tired* she bends her head and rests her face in her hands. She stays in this gesture for a short time.

18. *Mary sings and rocks him mild...*

18. At *Mary sings* the educator lifts her head again and rests her hands in her lap. She softly hums the A note.

Continue with *Rocking* and *It is done*.

Journey to Egypt

Journey to Egypt may be played as a conclusion for the short Three Kings Play (Core Play) and also for the Complete Play, with its Supplementary Scenes.

At the start of the play it is revealed that the bright star above the house cannot be seen any more and also that the child cannot be found in the house. In a short review the children are led back once more to the event of the coming of the Three Kings in an active, imitative way, always asking the open question: 'What happened?' Then follows the dream of Joseph, the starting point of the flight to Egypt. The content of the play is formed so that the original dramatic event leading to the flight of the holy family can only be suspected. Then the children may dive into the action free of sorrow or fear. In Journey to Egypt, the long journey is the centre of the action. The play addition *Rest under the palm tree* may be inserted as desired. It uses the Choroi children's harp again, with its soothing sound.

The props for the Three Kings Play (star, throne, child, bells on a ring) are not needed for Journey to Egypt. But the children may be dressed in the tabard to tune them into the special play event.

Journey to Egypt play sequence

A. Prelude
  1. Outside and in the house
  2. Review

B. Main Play
  1. Dream and departure
  2. On the road and postlude

Play addition: *The holy family rests under the palm tree*

A. PRELUDE

1. Outside and in the house

> The star
> above the house in Bethlehem
> you cannot see it more.
> Where could it be?
> Come, come in to the house with me.
> We'll go and see.
>
> Oh, where is the little child?
> You cannot see him more!
> The little child, the little son,
> where has he gone?
> What happened on that night of yore?

2. Review

After the holy kings
had given to the Christ Child their
offerings,
the gold, the frankincense, and the
myrrh,
thankfully they travelled home again
to far Eastern lands.

At home, to soothe the little child
Mary sang and rocked him mild.

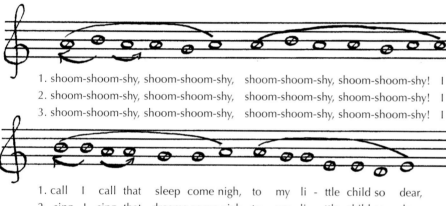

1. shoom-shoom-shy, shoom-shoom-shy,   shoom-shoom-shy, shoom-shoom-shy!   I
2. shoom-shoom-shy, shoom-shoom-shy,   shoom-shoom-shy, shoom-shoom-shy!   I
3. shoom-shoom-shy, shoom-shoom-shy,   shoom-shoom-shy, shoom-shoom-shy!   I

1. call   I   call that   sleep come nigh,   to   my   li - ttle child so   dear,
2. sing   I   sing that   dreams come nigh,   to   my   li - ttle child so   dear,
3. pray to   an - gels   to   come nigh,   to   my   li - ttle child so   dear,

B. MAIN PLAY

1. Dream and departure

Mary and the Jesus child
fell into a slumber deep.
Joseph, too, did sleep.
He had a dream!
An angel appeared to him
and called: "Joseph! Joseph!
With Mary and with Jesus small
quickly to Egypt travel all."

Joseph woke up right.
He got up in the night,
quickly went into the stall
bringing out the donkey small, the donkey small.
Mary took Jesus in her arms,
covered him with a blanket warm
and took her seat on the donkey small.

She said:
"Take me and my child, I pray,
quickly to Egypt land today."
The donkey called: "Hee-haw! Hee-haw!"
Pawed with his leg: scrapy-scrape,
and trotted along with gentle step,
and trotted along with gentle step.

2.   On the road and postlude

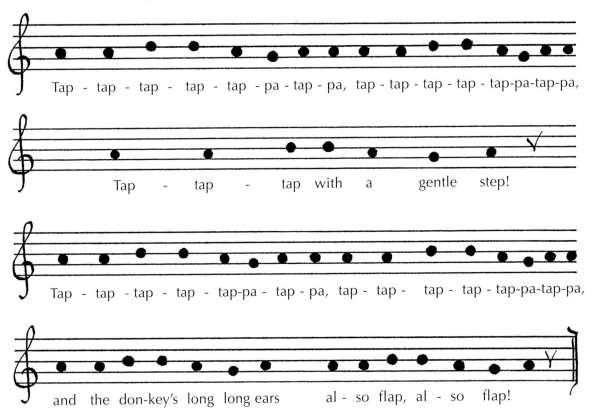

Tap - tap - tap - tap - tap - pa - tap - pa, tap - tap - tap - tap - tap-pa-tap-pa,

Tap - tap - tap with a gentle step!

Tap - tap - tap - tap - tap-pa - tap - pa, tap - tap - tap - tap - tap-pa-tap-pa,

and the don-key's long long ears al - so flap, al - so flap!

And Joseph walked with measured tread,
with measured tread and with firm step,
with measured step and tread
Joseph walked ahead.

The angel with his wings outspread
guided the holy family ahead,
walked unseen at their right hand
into holy Egypt land.
Guided, guided,
to Egypt land.

The house in Bethlehem is empty!
Joseph, Mary and the child so small
we cannot find them there at all.
To Egypt land they travel on.
From the house they now are gone
and our play is done!

It is done.

A. PRELUDE

1. Outside and in the house

1. *The star...*

1. Children and educator are standing in a circle. For the star gesture the educator moves her right hand, palm to the observer, in front of the palm of her left hand. The fingers of both palms are spread. Once her left hand lies on the back of her right hand she pushes the fingers of her left hand through the gaps of the spread fingers of her right hand. She lifts her hands above her head a little and keeps them there for a while.

2. *above the house in Bethlehem…*

2. The educator makes a roof with her hands and arms.

3. *you cannot see it more…*

3. With her hands against her forehead like a visor, the educator looks up to the sky.

4. *Where could it be?*

4. Holding the same gesture, she searches the sky from left to right.

5. *Come, come into the house with me…*

5. At the word *come* the educator lowers her hands, looks at the children and waves in an inviting gesture. At *go into the house with me* she shows the house roof again (see 2).

6. (Silent)	6. Very slowly, she lowers her arms.
7. *We go and see…*	7. The educator takes two cautious steps to the circle centre, first with her right, the second with her left foot, as if expecting to find the child in the house.
8. *Oh, where is the little child?*	8. At *Oh* she points to the spot where the throne with the child stood in the Three Kings Play. At *where is the little child?* she moves her hands back and up in a questioning gesture.
9. *You cannot see him more!*	9. Shielding her forehead with both hands, she looks at the empty spot.
10. *The little child, the little son…*	10. With joined arms she makes rocking movements.
11. *Where has he gone?*	11. Again, the educator moves her hands to her forehead like a visor, and searches the room another time. Her gesture and voice express her amazement but are free of expressions like fear or sorrow.
12. *What happened on that night of yore?*	12. The educator clasps her hands in front of her chest as she asks the question.

At this point one may continue directly with the Core Play.
The following scene, *Review*, reminds the children of key events in the Three Kings Play.

2. Review

1. *After the holy kings...*

2. *had given to the Christ Child...*

3. *their offerings...*

4. *gold...*

1. The educator forms a crown on her head using her hands.

2. She dissolves the crown gesture and lowers her arms to her sides. Then she raises her arms to chest height, turning her palms up to show two offering bowls (her fingers point to the observers).

3. She continues as in 2. Then she lowers her hands and bows.

4. She joins her hands at the fingertips so they become *one* offering bowl. She holds this gesture for a while.

5. *frankin cense... (silent)*
   ↑ ↓ ↑ ↓
   (forwards) (back) (forwards)(back)

5. The educator holds her hands upward, her fingertips and the balls of her hands touching. There is a hollow space between both hands with gaps between her fingers so that smoke might escape. She swings her hands back and forth in the given rhythm.

6. *and myrrh...*

6. Now the educator builds a box with lid with both hands. With her left hand she forms a deep bowl. She does the same with her right hand, with the back of her hand up. She now puts her right hand as a 'lid' on her left hand.

7. *they thankfully travelled home again...*

7. At *thankfully*, she crosses her hands at the wrists and lays them on her chest, bowing her head. At *travelled home* she points with both hands over the top to the right.

8. *to the far Eastern lands...*

8. She points again to the right.

9. *At home, to soothe the little child...*

9. The educator shows the roof. At *to soothe the little child* she sits down again on her heels and rests her face in her hands.

10. *Mary sang...*	10. Now she kneels up, resting her hands loosely on her thighs.
11. *and rocked him mild...*	11. The educator joins her arms and rocks the imaginary child. She hums the note A while rocking.

Now continue with *Rocking*, then continue with the Core Play.

B. MAIN PLAY

1. Dream and departure

1. *Mary and the Jesus child*	1. After the educator has finished the song, she silently rocks the imaginary child once more. Only then does she speak: "Mary and the Jesus child"
2. *Fell into a slumber deep...*	2. Still on her knees, she joins her hands and snuggles her left cheek into them. She holds this gesture for a while.

3.   *Joseph, too, did sleep…*

3.   She puts her hands by her ears, her head lightly bent, her eyes lowered. She holds this gesture for a while.

4.   *He had a dream!*

4.   The educator raises her head from her hands, still looking down. She holds this gesture for a while.

5. *An angel appeared to him...*

6. *and called: "Joseph! Joseph!"*

7. *With Mary and with Jesus small...*
   (forwards)   (back)

8. *quickly to Egypt travel all...*

9. *Joseph woke up right...*

10. *He got up in the night...*

5. She rises to a knee stand, lifting up her arms as wings.

6. She calls Joseph cautiously by name. The educator speaks in a melody from low to high pitch: *Jo...* in a dark voice, *...seph!* in a light voice.

7. She moves her wings very lightly forward at *Mary* and back at *Jesus*.

8. The educator is still holding the angel gesture. At *Egypt* she makes a large wing movement forwards and up. She speaks the word *Egypt* very slowly. Then she makes a small backward movement with her hands. She holds the wings still for a while.

9. The educator rubs her eyes.

10. She stands up.

11. *quickly went into the stall…*

11. She takes two small steps into the centre of the room.

12. *bringing out the donkey small…*

12. She grasps an imaginary rope with her hands to pull out the imaginary donkey. She takes two small steps back.

13. *the donkey small…*

13. The educator puts her hands against her head as ears. At *donkey* she bends her head lightly and tips her 'ears' forwards a little.

14. *Mary took Jesus in her arms…*

14. The educator holds the imaginary child in her left arm.

15. *covered him with a blanket warm…*

15. With her right arm she spreads an imaginary blanket around the child, so she holds him covered up.

16. *and took her seat on the donkey small…*

16. With the child on her arm, the educator 'sits' by slightly bending her knees twice.

17. *She said:*
    "Take me and my child, I pray,
    quickly to Egypt land today."

17. After the second knee bend the educator remains in the assumed seating gesture, the child in her arm. In this gesture she says *Take me*. By the words *I pray* and *Egypt land*, she nods.

18. *The donkey called: "Hee-haw! Hee-haw!"*

18. Then the educator puts her hands against her head as ears again. For the *hee-haw* call she stretches a little at *hee*, then leans her head a little forward and down at *haw*.

19. *Pawed with his leg: scrapy-scrape...*

19. The educator puts her hands at her chest and scrapes across the floor with her right foot. This may be repeated.

20. *and trotted along with gentle step,*
     and trotted along with gentle step.

20. The educator makes a quarter turn with her right shoulder to the circle centre. She starts to trot along the circle on the balls of her feet, lightly and in moderate tempo. At each step she pulls up her knees a little.

2. ON THE ROAD AND POSTLUDE

1. *Tap-tap-tap-tap-tappa, tappa... etc.*

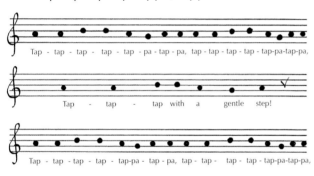

Tap - tap - tap - tap - tap - pa - tap - pa, tap - tap - tap - tap - tap-pa-tap-pa,

Tap - tap - tap with a gentle step!

Tap - tap - tap - tap - tap-pa - tap - pa, tap - tap - tap - tap - tap-pa-tap-pa,

1. The educator continues to trot as a donkey along the circle. She takes one step to each note. For the children, steps and rhythm do not need to match. By the time children are approaching first grade there often is an enthusiastic attempt to step in time. This should be allowed without calling attention to it.

2. *long long ears, they also flap!*
    (down)   (up)   (down)

and the don-key's long long ears   al - so flap, al - so   flap!

2. At *and the ears* she puts her hands against her head and moves them as noted under the text. She still trots along, but slows down with the singing and movements, then comes to a stop.

3. *long long ears, they also flap!*
   (up)   (down)   (up) (down)

3. At the repeated line, she flaps her ears while standing. The singing gets slower and the hand gestures slow down accordingly.

4. *And Joseph walked with measured tread,*
   with measured tread and with firm step,
   with measured step and tread
   Joseph walked ahead.

4. The educator straightens, her arms hanging by her sides. She walks on with long, firm steps. Each underlined syllable corresponds to one step. (Conforming is not necessary for the children.)

5. The angel with his wings outspread
   guided the holy   family   ahead...
   (forward) (back) (forward) (back)
   walked unseen at their right   hand...
   (forward) (back) (forward)   (back)
   into   holy   Egypt   land...
   (forward) (back) (forward) (back)
   Guided... (silent movement)
   (forward)   (back)
   guided... (silent movement)
   (forward)   (back)
   into holy Egypt land.
   (forward) (back) (forward) (back)

5. The educator lifts her arms as 'wings' and then continues along the circle in light, gliding steps while moving the wings lightly forward and back. The arm movements are slow and quiet.

The play addition *The holy family rests under the palm tree* may be inserted here.

6. (Silent movement)

6. Slowly the educator comes to a standstill and waits until all the children have stopped. Then she lowers her arms and turns her face to the circle centre. She takes pauses.

7. *The house in Bethlehem is empty!*

7. At *house* she forms a roof, at *empty* she shows her empty hands.

8. *Joseph, Mary and the child so small...*

8. At *Joseph* the educator stands up straight, then bows while moving her hands back a little. At *Mary* she crosses her arms in front without touching her chest. At *the child* she holds her arms at the elbows and makes a cradle movement.

9. *we cannot find them there at all...*

9. She spreads her hands to show the empty room.

10. *To Egypt land they travel on...*

10. The educator points to the left with both hands raised up high.

11. *From the house they are now gone...*

11. She makes the gesture for the roof, then spreads her empty hands.

12. *and our play is done!*

12. She slowly lowers her arms and lets them hang by her sides.

13.

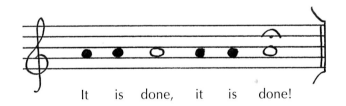

It   is   done,   it   is   done!

13. The educator strikes the cymbals, moves them apart and back together and sings *It is done!* Repeat the ceremony.

Journey to Egypt: Play Addition

THE HOLY FAMILY RESTS UNDER THE PALM TREE

Arrived in Egypt land
they all stopped to rest.
Joseph, Mary with the child,
and also the donkey small.
Under the palm tree,
under the palm tree they stopped to rest.
The angel guarded their dream.
He took his heavenly harp
and softly played for the three
a dream melody.

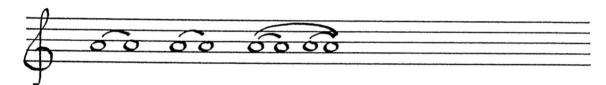

Spoken: *A dream melody*

Of what did they dream then?
They dreamt of Bethlehem
of the place
from which they all had set their pace
to Egypt land, to Egypt land.

1.	*Arrived in Egypt land…*	1.	The educator comes to a standstill with her arms held high as 'wings'. She waits until all children are standing, too.

2.	*they all stopped to rest…*	2.	She now dissolves the angel gesture, lowers her arms to her sides and nods lightly at *rest*.
3.	*Joseph…*	3.	At *Joseph* she bows, the palms of her hands by her side turned to the observer. When she bends her upper body, her arms move back a little.
4.	*Mary…*	4.	At *Mary* the educator crosses her arms in front of her chest. Her arms should not touch her chest.

5.	*with the child...*	5.	The educator puts her lower arms together, right arm nearest the observers. She holds an imaginary child in her arms, rocking it once to the left and once to right.
6.	*and also the donkey small...*	6.	At *the donkey* she puts her hands against her chest as hooves.
7.	*Under the palm tree...*	7.	The educator lifts her arms and hangs her hands down in front as hanging palm leaves (not too high).

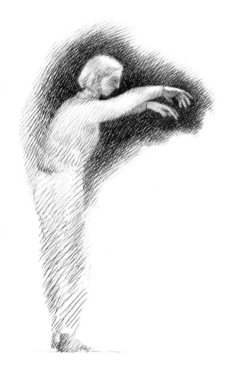

8.	*under the palm tree...*	8.	The educator swings her upper body a little, forwards and back as if blown by a soft wind.

9. *they stopped to rest...*	9. She takes her arms down and at the same time lowers herself slowly into the knee stand. Her arms hang beside her body, her head is slightly bent.
10. *The angel guarded...*	10. Still in the knee stand, the educator lifts up her arms in the angel gesture. At *guarded*, she moves the wings forward a little to form a sheltering gesture. She holds this gesture for a while.
11. *their dream...*	11. She sits down on her heels, puts her hands against her cheek and at *dream* she snuggles her slightly raised face into her hands. She is looking down. She holds this gesture for a while.
12. *He took his heavenly harp...*	12 The educator picks up the Choroi children's harp. She sets herself in position to play; this can be sitting on her heels, or on a stool or chair. Then she gently plays the note A.
13. *and softly played for the three a dream melody.*	13. At *a dream melody*, she rests her slightly bent head on her right hand.
14.	14. She plays the dream melody. After each note she raises her hand, drawing attention to the tone. Meanwhile she listens after each note. This way she makes the sound experience clear for the children through physical gesture.

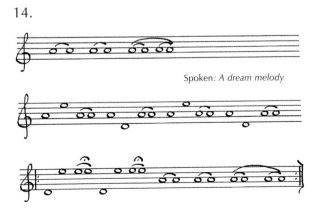

Spoken: *A dream melody*

166

15. (Silent)

15. The educator puts the harp away, slowly and quietly.

16. (Silent)

16. After the educator has put away the harp she makes the dream gesture again: her face turned lightly upwards, eyes half closed, snuggled into her hands. Sitting on her heels, she remains in this gesture for a while.

17. *Of what did they dream then?*

17. She asks the words *Of what did they dream then?* softly. She remains in the dream gesture with lowered eyes.

18. *They dreamt of Bethlehem...*

18. She opens her eyes, rises into the knee stand and raises both arms in an upward arc.

19. *of the place...*

19. She joins her fingers above her head to form a roof.

20. *from which they all had set their pace...*

20. She brings her hands down. Then she shows her empty hands as if to show that the house really is empty. At *all* she brings her hands to her head, and then in a large arc forward, pointing far away.

21. *to Egypt land, to Egypt land…*

21. The educator points with both hands in a high arc to the West.

From here, continue with 'Journey to Egypt', at *in Bethlehem the house is empty…*

Extended dream melody:

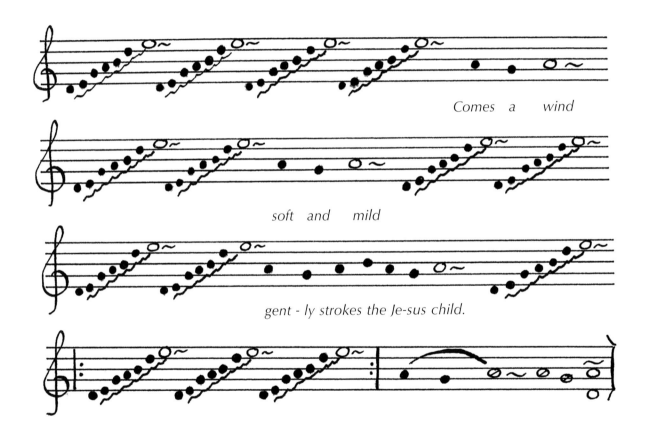

Comes a wind

soft and mild

gent - ly strokes the Je-sus child.

Sewing and Craft Directions

For both plays

Tabard

Tabard material
- Silk, wool-silk mix, or cotton fabric, 60 cm (25 in) long and 1.2 m (4 ft) wide – this will make two tabards

Cutting instructions
- Lay the fabric out with the fold at the top, leaving a little extra at the bottom to allow for a hem. For the side seams, allow an extra 1.5 cm (½ in). For the neck opening, no allowance needs to be made for a seam.

Sewing instructions
- Use a sewing machine to sew the side seams.
- At the sleeve openings, fold the extra seam allowance to the inside and sew together.
- Close the neck opening with bias tape.

Belt

Belt material
- The same material as for the tabard, 80 cm (2 ½ ft) long and 9 cm (4 in) wide.
- For colour suggestions see p. 11

Sewing instructions
- For the belt, sew together one length, turn and on the opposite length, fold the fabric inside and sew by hand, as neatly as possible.

Pocket for the silver cymbals

Material
- Felt (any colour apart from black and white)

Sewing instructions
- Cut a strip 27 cm (10 in) long and 7 cm (3 in) wide.
- Fold turn in 6 cm (2 in) from both sides and sew them together with a buttonhole stitch along the length.
- Alternatively, use another decorative stitch with a sewing machine.

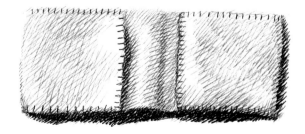

For the Shepherds Play

Jesus child

Very young children do not yet have free conceptions but conceptions based on perceptions. It is therefore essential that the Jesus child can be physically perceived, without being naturalistic or doll-like.

The Jesus child of the gospel of St Luke, the centre of Shepherds Play, is usually represented lying down in paintings or stone relief. In the Romanesque period, the child is swaddled in a wheat-ear pattern.

Materials
- Cotton jersey fabric, close to Caucasian skin colour, 80 x 80 cm (30 x 30 in)
- 3 m (9 ft) of another fabric, such as wool, linen or cotton, in a neutral colour, cut into strips roughly 7 cm (3 in) wide
- 150–200 g (5-7 oz) carded wool fleece

Instructions
- Roll two thirds of the fleece into a medium tight ball and put it into the middle of the square cloth.
- Cover the wool with the cotton jersey cloth and wrap the cloth under the wool tightly with a small portion of the fabric strips.
- Put the rest of the wool loosely into the piece of square cloth hanging down and wrap it with the strips.
- Bind the uppermost layer of the wrapping crosswise, so as to make the wheat-ear pattern.

Manger

- Spread a brown cloth, 1 x 1 m (3 x 3 ft) on the floor. On it lay straw (and hay, if available) in an oval. Baby Jesus is put on top. At first he is covered with a light green cloth. (The cloth may also be in a darker skin colour.)

The simple manger
- Cover the inside of a basket or a box with a brown cloth, put hay and straw inside and set it on a low stool. Put the baby in it (first covered by a light green cloth) so that it can easily be seen.

The formed manger
- A wooden manger with straight or slanting sides should be fixed in place so it cannot move. This is filled with hay and straw and the baby, first covered with the light green cloth, is placed inside.

Jingle stick

Materials
- Dowel, 1.5 cm (½ in) diameter, length 16–20 cm (6–8 in)
- Raffia in two colours, or colourful border braid, about 1.5 cm (½ in) wide
- 4 small bells, two with a diameter of 1 cm (½ in) and two with a diameter of 1.5 cm (¾ in)
- Hat elastic

Instructions

- Cut dowel to the right length, smoothing the ends with sandpaper.
- Drill holes through the dowel, 2.5 cm and 5.5 cm (1 in and 2 in) from the dowel end.
- Braid the raffia, 12 threads from each colour, each 25 cm (10 in) long.
- Tie all threads tightly together at one end, divide into three groups and plait. Tie the finished braid at the lower end.
- Position the middle of the braid on the upper dowel end so that the two ends lie on top of the drilled holes. Tie the braid to the stick in two places, using a piece of raffia (see image).

Note: There are two kinds of jingle bells: some with metal balls, and some with pebbles. For the jingle sticks, jingles with metal balls are recommended. No larger jingles should be used. Their sound would be too loud and overwhelming.

For the Three Kings Play

Jesus child

The Jesus child in the gospel of St Matthew is portrayed sitting in all representations. This is a suggestion for us.

Materials
- Light yellow silk, 80 x 80 cm (30 x 30 in)
- Tie from the same fabric, 30 x 2.5 cm (11 x 1 in)
- Yellow wool yarn, 50 cm (20 in)
- Gold braid, as narrow as possible, 50 cm (20 in)
- 50–75 g (2–3 oz) unspun wool

Instructions
- Put a ball of unspun wool in the middle of the square fabric. The ball is rolled quite tightly.
- Pull the fabric around the ball as smoothly as possible and tie it with the tie. This is done as carefully as possible, for this will be visible as the child's neck.
- Tie the narrow gold braid round the head as a crown.
- Take each end of the hanging fabric, wrap it around some unspun wool and bind off the end with wool yarn as hands. Let the rest of the fabric hang down.
- Now set the child on a throne.

Throne

- An oval or round basket can be made into a throne. Put a pillow inside. Pillow and basket are covered with a blue silk cloth. On this the royal child is sat, so that the head can lean against the rim of the basket and the hands have some support at the sides. Drape part of the fabric over the edges of the basket. It is best to put the basket on a low stool covered with a yellow or blue cloth. For the start of the play, the Jesus child is covered with a small silk cloth. Only when the kings enter the house is the cloth removed. The basket must be positioned so that the Jesus child looks at the circle centre.

Star

- Use cardboard for the six-sided (or eight-sided) star, glued on both sides with gold foil.
- Make a small round wrap out of the middle of a toilet roll to fasten it to the staff. To do this, cut the cardboard open lengthwise and cut off a piece 3 cm (1 in) wide. This is wrapped around the staff and glued in place.
- This wrap is also covered with gold foil.
- A cover for the wrap can be made out of the gold foil so it sits securely on top of the staff. Then the wrap will be glued on to the star's back.
- As a star holder, use a large vase or bottle filled with sand or a large flower pot standing on the ground with its wide side. The hole in the flowerpot must be adapted to the diameter of the staff.

Small bell on a ring

Materials
- 1 brass bell with metal tongue inside, 28 mm (1 in) diameter
- 1 wooden ring, 37 mm (1½ in) diameter
- Strong cotton thread/yarn, 50 cm (20 in) long

Note: Bells are available in craft stores or Waldorf school stores. Wooden rings can be bought from DIY stores or home improvement centres.

Instructions
- Pull the thread through the eye of the bell so that the bell hangs in the middle of the thread. Tie a double knot.
- Thread one of the yarn ends through the eye, repeat, threading in the same direction, then knot it at the end.
- Repeat this procedure in the opposite direction, then knot it at the other yarn end.

- Now wrap the two yarn ends around the ring several times in opposite directions, pull very tightly and knot it on the inside of the ring.
- Take the two ends from the inside and wrap them tightly from opposite directions around the space between the bell and the eye. Do this several times, pulling and knotting them very tightly.
- The bell must be tied against the ring so that it cannot move independently when it is being swung it. If it does still swing, continue wrapping and tying the yarn until the bell is completely tight against the ring. Then cut the rest of the yarn ends.

Index of Songs

Further Reading

Also by Wilma Ellersiek

Dancing Hand, Trotting Pony: Hand Gesture Games, Songs and Movement Games for Children in Kindergarten and the Lower Grades

Gesture Games for Spring and Summer: Hand Gesture, Song and Movement Games for Children in Kindergarten and the Lower Grades

Gesture Games for Autumn and Winter: Hand Gesture, Song and Movement Games for Children in Kindergarten and the Lower Grades

Gesture Games for Spring, Summer, Autumn and Winter: A Learning CD

Giving Love, Bringing Joy: Hand Gesture Games and Lullabies in the Mood of the Fifth, for Children Between Birth and Nine

Giving Love, Bringing Joy: A Learning CD

All published by the Waldorf Early Childhood Association of North America

You may also be interested in –

Barnes, Diane Ingraham, *Music Through the Grades in the Light of the Developing Child*, Adonis Press

Bernstein, Steve, *Recorder Ensemble: First Collection for Soprano, Alto, Tenor and Bass*, Association of Waldorf Schools of North America

Foster, Nancy, The *Mood of the Fifth: A Musical Approach to Early Childhood*, Waldorf Early Childhood Association North America

Lonsky, Karen, *A Day Full of Song (Book & CD)*, Waldorf Early Childhood Association North America

Masters, Brian, *The Waldorf Song Book*, Floris Books

Moore, Richard, *Five Plays for Waldorf Festivals*, Steiner Waldorf Schools Fellowship

Preston, Michael, *Music from Around the World for Recorders: Ensemble Music for Descant, Alto and Tenor Recorders in Waldorf Schools*, Association of Waldorf Schools of North America

Spence, Roswitha, *Clothing the Play: The Art and Craft of Stage Design*, Association of Waldorf Schools of North America

Willwerth, Ilian, *Merrily We Sing: Original Songs in the Mood of the Fifth*, Waldorf Early Childhood Association North America

Zahlingen, Bronja, *Lifetime of Joy: A Collection of Circle Games, Finger Games, Songs, Verses and Plays for Puppets and Marionettes*, Waldorf Early Childhood Association North America

Making a Nativity Scene

Christmas Figures and Animals for a Seasonal Display

Viola Ulke

The Christmas Craft Book

Thomas Berger

The Advent Craft and Activity Book

Stories, crafts, recipes and poems for the Christmas season

Christel Dhom

A SWEDISH CHRISTMAS

Simple Scandinavian Crafts, Recipes and Decorations

CAROLINE WENDT AND PERNILLA WASTBERG

www.florisbooks.co.uk

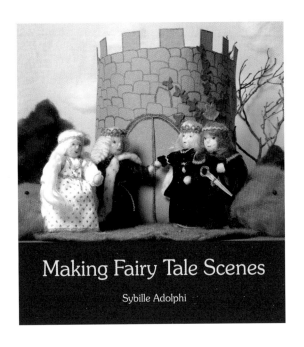

Making Fairy Tale Scenes

Sybille Adolphi

Crafts Through the Year

Thomas and Petra Berger

Magical Window Stars

Frédérique Guéret

Magic Wool Fairies

Christine Schäfer

www.florisbooks.co.uk